10-Minute Stories From Greek Mythology: The Iliad And The Odyssey

Timeless Legendary Tales To Inspire Kids Of All Ages

Joy Chester

Copyright © 2023 by Joy Chester

All rights reserved. No part of this publication may be reproduced, stored or transmitted in any form or by any means, electronic, mechanical, photocopying, recording, or otherwise without written permission from the publisher. It is illegal to copy this book, post it to a website, or distribute it by any other means without permission.

Joy Chester asserts the moral right to be identified as the author of this work.

Joy Chester has no responsibility for the persistence or accuracy of URIs for external or third-party Internet Websites referred to in this publication and does not guarantee that any content on such Websites is, or will remain, accurate or appropriate.

Designation used by companies to distinguish their products are often claimed as trademarks. All brand names and product names used in this book and on its cover are trade names, service marks, trademarks and registered trademarks of their respective owners. The publishers and the book are not associated with any product or vendor mentioned in this book. None of the companies referenced within the book have endorsed the book.

TABLE OF CONTENTS

Preface v

PART I
THE ROAD TO WAR

Chapter 1: The Judgement of Paris 2

Chapter 2: Laomedon and Herakles 9

Chapter 3: Helen of Sparta 16

Chapter 4: The Greeks Assemble 23

Chapter 5: The Greeks sail for Troy. 30

PART II
THE TROJAN WAR

Chapter 1: An Archer, a Prophecy, and a Curse 39

Chapter 2: Agamemnon dishonors Achilles 45

Chapter 3: The Fight between Menelaus and Paris 51

Chapter 4: The Duels of Hector 57

Chapter 5: Achilles versus Hector 64

PART III
THE FALL OF TROY

Chapter 1: The Grief of King Priam 72

Chapter 2: The Deaths of Achilles and Paris 78

Chapter 3: The Madness of Ajax.. 85

Chapter 4: The Wooden Horse 91

Chapter 5: Aeneas' Flight from Troy 97

PART IV
THE ADVENTURES OF ODYSSEUS

Chapter 1: Polyphemus.. 105

Chapter 2: The Bag of Winds 113

Chapter 3: Circe... 119

Chapter 4: Odysseus in the Underworld 125

Chapter 5: The Sirens, Scylla, and Charybdis................. 132

Chapter 6: The Island of Helios 139

Chapter 7: Calypso 145

Chapter 8: The Suitors... 152

Chapter 9: Penelope... 158

Chapter 10: The Trial of Axes 163

Glossary.. 169

PREFACE

Children nowadays seem to read less and less. Reading a book can seem like a chore when entertainment can be gained through a screen so much more easily. But studies have shown that developing an "atomic habit" - just doing ten minutes a day of whatever skill or habit you want to take on can be more than enough to engrain it into our lives. Therefore, we have transformed timeless, legendary stories into 10-minute, bite-size chunks long enough to entertain, enthrall, and even educate the reader but short enough to be enjoyed quickly at bedtime or any other time in our busy modern days. Within weeks, reading just 10 minutes a day, children can develop a habit that will benefit their lives immeasurably. It starts with just the turn of a page.

This book contains some of the oldest stories in the world. Around 2,700 years ago, a man called Homer (not Simpson) sat down and pulled together the various stories that had been told around firesides for years and years. We know them as the Iliad and the Odyssey. He wanted to record these tales so that they would not be forgotten. He succeeded. We're just the latest in a long line of authors who have been captured by these epic tales and decided to give these old stories a new feeling.

Why did we do it? Why have these stories lasted so long? Because these are not just the oldest stories known but also among the greatest. They are tales of heroes and monsters, gods and magic, mysterious islands and grand cities. Everyone may have heard of Achilles and Hector, Herakles and Odysseus. They were the first superheroes, along with all the others whose stories have echoed down the ages to us. They set the standard for every hero who came after. Without Herakles, we would not have had Superman.

Therefore, we decided to bring a new edition of these stories into the world, designed for younger readers. To help give the stories and characters a bit more context, we have started with stories from before the Trojan War (e.g., Herakles and Laomedon). Each chapter can stand alone or be read in order. You could enjoy them at bedtime, in the car, on a plane, wherever you like. That's the magic of these tales; you can take them anywhere! Some of the more gruesome or difficult details have been left aside, lying ready in the original texts for the adventurous soul who wants to dive in, having been hooked by the gripping tales in this book. That's the hope, anyway. As already said, these are some of the greatest stories ever told. There is a whole world out there, ready to be discovered.

So, reader, be ready to be thrilled, excited, scared, disgusted, confused, enthralled, and delighted. We truly envy you because you are about to read these stories for the very first time, and that is a special moment. Take a deep breath and dive on in.

Part I

The Road to War

CHAPTER 1

The Judgement of Paris

Long ago, there lived a sea nymph called Thetis. Like all nymphs, she was beautiful, and like many beautiful women, she caught the eye of Zeus, king of the gods. But Zeus had learned of a prophecy foretold that Thetis's son would be greater than his father. Fearing what would happen if any immortal were to father a child with her, Zeus decided that she should marry his mortal grandson Peleus.

The wedding took place on the slopes of Mount Olympus, for no human may set foot in the gods' palace. It was a happy affair, and all the gods brought gifts for the couple. Everyone was having a good time until a shadow darkened the door. Silence hushed the crowd as in walked Eris, goddess of discord and strife. "I, too, have something to offer!" She cried gleefully. Then she laid an apple made of pure gold on the floor and departed, still laughing. Upon the apple's surface was written: "for the most beautiful". With one movement, Athene, the goddess of war, Hera, the queen of the gods, and Aphrodite, the goddess of love, all reached out for the golden fruit. The next moment, they had turned on each other, each demanding the apple for themselves. Zeus, slamming his goblet down on the table, pulled the three apart.

"Even I shall not decide this!" He decided.

"Then who, husband?" demanded Hera, her hands on her hips.

"There is a man, Paris of Troy." Explained Zeus. "Paris' mother, the queen of Troy, dreamt, the night of his birth, that instead of a baby, she had given birth to a flaming torch which burnt Troy to the ground. So, when Paris was born, King Priam ordered his servant Agelaus to take the baby boy away and kill him. But the man could not do it and so simply left Paris out on the slopes of Mount Ida to die. On returning to the spot a few days later, Agelaus found that a mother bear had taken care of the boy. Taking this as a sign, Agelaus raised the boy as his own son.

"Years later, Paris was helping his father herd theprized bulls of Troy, gifts from the gods andinvincible. Then, another great bull came up theslopes of Mount Ida, Ares in disguise– not that Paris knew this. Ares challenged Paris' champion bull, and the two struggled for a long time. But ultimately, Paris awarded the victory to the unknown bull. Ares admired the young man's honest judgement and brought word of it back to Olympus."

Zeus paused before continuing.

"That is who shall decide,

dear wife: A mortal man who has no reason to give a false judgement. Go to him, now."

So it was that, while Paris was sitting on the slopes of Mount Ida, the three goddesses, Athene, Hera, and Aphrodite, appeared before him and demanded that he award the golden apple to the one he judged to be the most beautiful.

"But how can I choose?" Asked Paris. "You are all beautiful, and I am just a mortal man!"

"Nevertheless," replied Hera, "You must choose."

Paris bit his lip and looked at each goddess in turn.

Athene was the tallest. She had tied her raven-black hair in a tight bun. She wore armor, and her deep, dark eyes regarded him silently. She was a striking woman, no mistake.

Aphrodite was as fair as Athene was not. She wore her long, blonde hair loose, and it waved gently in the breeze. Though slightly shorter than Athene and Hera, her smile was haunting and reached up to her eyes, blue as a lagoon.

Hera did not look older than the other two. The crown she wore framed her auburn hair magnificently, and Paris found it hard to look away from her. He wasn't sure if he felt fear or not when she looked at him.

Heart pounding in his chest, Paris spoke. "I cannot decide right this second. Give me a day. Tomorrow we shall meet again on this spot, and I shall choose who gets the golden apple."

Athene, Hera, and Aphrodite glanced at each other and then nodded. Paris breathed easy again.

Hera handed him the golden apple. "Until tomorrow, son of Troy."

A gust of wind shook the tree branches behind him, blowing dust into his face. In the instant it took to brush his eyes clean, all three goddesses had disappeared.

Paris weighed the golden apple in his hands. How could he choose?

"I don't envy you this choice, Paris." A kindly voice said behind him. He turned quickly.

Athene leaned against the tree, plucking an olive from the branch and regarding it before popping it into her mouth.

Paris stared at her; mouth slightly open.

"You know that I am the goddess of wisdom." Continued Athene, smiling down at him. "So let me help you with your difficulties. If you choose me and hand me the golden apple tomorrow morning, I shall grant you such skills in judgment, foresight, and understanding that no man on earth will surpass you. Kings and emperors will come to you for advice. The whole world shall know Paris, wisest of all men."

A wonderful image played through Paris' mind. He was neither the fastest of his friends nor the strongest. But if he could outwit his friends and his foes, if he could be the most intelligent man ever, imagine what he could accomplish! He looked up at Athene, but she had gone. He stood and plucked an olive as well. He stared down at its black flesh, which seemed almost grey compared with Athene's raven-dark hair. Tossing it aside, he hefted the golden apple into his bag and went home.

That evening, Paris sat alone in his room, his heart weighed down by the judgment just as his bag was by the apple. He jumped as someone knocked at the door.

"Come in!" He called.

The warm fragrance of the sea wafted in as golden-haired Aphrodite stepped lightly through the door. Leaping to his feet, his face red, Paris stuttered. "My lady of Cyprus, I…"

She waved a hand to silence him, smiling that haunting smile. She sat daintily on the edge of his bed. "Paris…" Her voice was as soft as the foam on a wave when it hushed over the sand. "I see you, noble and fair, here all alone. It must be so hard for you, young though you are. Hear my offer: Judge me the fairest, and I will give you the love of the most beautiful woman in the world. She shall be yours, and you shall be happy."

Again, as though through a window, Paris saw himself sitting on a grassy slope, hand in hand with a beautiful woman who smiled up at him. Gorgeous, happy children ran up and down and around, laughing and singing in the sunlight. Again, the vision faded, and Paris found himself alone in his room.

The following day, Paris woke early. So early that Aurora, the dawn goddess, had barely brought her rosy light to warm his windowsill. He left the house, wandering through the city. The streets were deserted as he climbed up to the walls to view the morning unfold.

"I know what you desire, young man." Said a regal voice from his right. Hardly surprised, he turned to face Hera's deep brown eyes and queenly face.

"There is more to you than you know." said Hera, "Have you never once thought whether you, too, could rule? Imagine it, to become more than just a shepherd. To know glory and power."

Paris bowed his head. He knew this but had never admitted it to himself. He felt Hera's hand brush his shoulder as she waved her arm out over the vista before them. "Give me the apple," she whispered. "And you shall have your own kingdom. Men shall flock to your banner, and your name will be held among the greatest on earth."

Paris could see the spears, hear the marching and singing of his armies, and see the city's walls as though carved by giants. Another gust of wind told him that Hera was gone.

Walking back up the hillside, Paris saw the three goddesses waiting for him. He took a deep breath and joined them under the olive tree. Paris looked at each of them in turn, Owl-eyed Athene; Hera, tall and proud;

Aphrodite with her hair wafting in the breeze. He thought of the gifts each had offered.

Without a word, he drew the apple from the bag and presented it to Aphrodite. She laughed raucously and seized it as the other two stamped their feet in rage.

"Thank you, Paris!" She crowed. "I shall not forget this nor our bargain."

"Nor shall we forget, boy." Hissed Hera, her eyes flashing. Athene nodded, and she now looked terrible in her beauty, fearsome to behold. Another flash of light and all three disappeared.

CHAPTER 2

Laomedon and Herakles

>>>> · <<<<

More than ten years had passed since Paris had chosen to give Aphrodite the golden apple, and he had long since forgotten about her promise. He had something else to occupy him, however, as this year he was old enough to enter the great annual bull-fighting tournament. Agelaus looked on proudly as his adopted son made his way through the competition. The final contest took place before all the citizens and the whole royal family. There was Priam, now an elderly king; Hecuba, old but still beautiful; Hector, the eldest son, mighty of arm and noble of spirit; and Cassandra, blessed with the gift of prophecy but cursed that no one ever believed her.

As the dust settled on the final bout, one man remained standing: Paris. Triumphant, he ascended the stands to receive his trophy from the king himself. Priam had to blink as the young man stood before him, covered in sweat, dust, and blood. The eyes were those of Cassandra, the build of his brother Hector, although Paris was a little shorter. But Paris' face could have been Priam's own when he was a boy. Priam stared at the man for a long moment.

"How can this be?" He wondered, and then his eyes fell on the boy's father, Agelaus, who stood nervously behind him. "Agelaus..." Priam asked. "Is this the boy I told you to take away when he was born?"

Fearing the king's wrath, Agelaus nodded nervously.

Priam's face broke into a wide smile. "Thank the gods that you didn't carry out my orders! Welcome Paris! Welcome home, prince of Troy!"

Though still rejoicing at the return of his lost son, Priam was reminded of a sadness that had long haunted him: his lost younger sister, Hesione. Years ago, his father, King Laomedon, sought the help of the gods Apollo and Poseidon to build the outer walls of Troy. In return, Laomedon promised to give them the invincible bulls gifted to him by the gods. But when the two gods had completed the work, Laomedon broke his promise and turned them away. Angered at the insult, the two gods sent a giant sea serpent to Troy. This serpent destroyed or scared off every ship that came near and caused huge waves to wash over the green fields of Ilium, slowly killing all the crops and drowning the livestock. When the king asked his priests what could be done about this monster, they replied that only the sacrifice of his daughter to the sea serpent would be enough. Thus, with a heavy heart, Laomedon took his daughter out to the rocks at the end of the bay of Troy's harbor, chained her, and returned to the city weeping.

Fortunately for Laomedon, who should happen to sail by at this moment, Herakles, son of Zeus, the strongest man, and the greatest hero the world had ever seen. Herakles was on his way back from the island of the Amazons with his friend and helper, Telamon. They had seen the beautiful princess tied to the rocks and came to offer their aid to the unhappy king. Laomedon was surprised and awed to meet so great a hero.

"Word has reached us here of your great labors, Herakles!" He cried, standing to welcome the colossal hero into his hall. "But I had not dared hope that you were even near Ilium! Do you think that you can defeat this foul sea serpent?"

Herakles rolled his massive shoulders and cracked his walnut-sized knuckles. "Lord king, I have caught the great Erymanthian Boar; slain the monstrous Hydra of Lernaea; and as you can see," he gestured to the lion skin he wore as a cloak, "even the Nemean Lion, called invulnerable by some, died at my hands. I shall defeat this snake too. But I have my price!"

Laomedon nodded; he had expected this. "I have a pair of horses, gifts to my father's father from the gods themselves. They are as swift as those that pull Apollo's chariot, but I would not ask you to test that!" He laughed nervously. "Save my daughter, rid my people of this foul sea-serpent, and the horses will be yours."

Herakles nodded his approval, hefted his massive club, and left the hall.

Telamon commanded their ship while Herakles wound the great anchor chain over his shoulder. Then they waited. The sea about them seemed calm enough, but Herakles knew the sea serpent had to be nearby. Suddenly, one of the sailors cried aloud and pointed. There, not two hundred paces off, the sea-serpent had surfaced, its great, ugly, triangular head pointed straight at them, the long coils of its body writhing as it zoomed towards them. "Telamon, raise sail and flee!" Cried Herakles, jumping up onto the side of the ship. "Flee for the land!" As the sea serpent came ever closer, Herakles leaped off the boat, hurling the anchor around its scaly neck. Somehow, he tied the chain tight before the creature dived into the depths.

The two struggled together for what seemed hours. The serpent smashed itself against rocks, leaped high out of the sea and back down again into the depths, and tried to wrap its horrible coils around its massive chest. But Herakles clung on, ever tightening the chain, sometimes managing even to give the creature a good whack across the face with his great club. Finally, when the chain was so tight that nothing could be seen but a red wheel across the serpent's flesh, the creature collapsed, unable to breathe. Taking his bright sword, Herakles hacked and hacked at the huge snake's neck until the head finally came free. Tired but triumphant, he swam with it back to Troy, where he was greeted with a hero's welcome.

That night, all of Troy feasted to celebrate the sea serpent's death and the princess's rescue. The next morning, Laomedon asked Herakles, with a heavy heart, if he was ready to take the horses.

"Thank you, my lord king," replied Herakles, "but I am still bound by oath to King Eurystheus to complete my labors. Until I am free, I will not take any property lest he demands it as his. Please look after my horses for me until I return."

With that, Herakles sailed away. Laomedon counted his blessings and ruled happily for many years. However, when the great hero finally returned to collect the horses, Laomedon refused to give him the rewards. He stood atop his great gates and laughed down at Herakles, saying, "You might now be free, mighty Herakles, and you might be strong, but the gods themselves built my walls! You are many things, but you are not stronger than the gods!"

Enraged, Herakles pounded the walls until they shook. "I shall return, liar Laomedon!" He spat. "And on that day, both my horses and your head shall be mine!"

It did not take long for Herakles to keep his word. Such was his fame across Greece for the great labors he had completed that many men flocked to his banner. He soon arrived back at Troy with 20 ships full of warriors. Such was

Herakles' strength that they quickly built a great siege tower and scaled the walls of Troy. Telamon was the first over the top, and together they led a terrible slaughter, for none dared face Herakles in all his might and fury. They defeated Troy's army, Laomedon's hopes were gone, and he barricaded himself and his family inside the palace. With four great strikes of his club, Herakles smashed the doors in and found Laomedon standing alone in armor, sword ready.

"You really expect to defeat me, liar Laomedon?" laughed the huge hero.

Laomedon shook his head. "No. But I can at least die well, even if I did not live well." With a cry, the old man charged Herakles head-on. A single sweep from his club and Herakles knocked Laomedon's shield aside like a slice of bread. A second sweep separated his head from his body.

The rest of Troy was spared. "You did not share your king's schemes." Herakles declared. "Although you may have profited from them."

With that, he gave Princess Hesione to his friend Telamon as a prize and turned to the young boy Priam, the last of Laomedon's children still living.

"I will not end this bloodline." The massive hero said. "But all Greece now knows of your father's betrayal, boy. Be better than him, or I shall return, and we shall test his boast about these walls."

Priam still remembered those words at night, echoing down the years. They still brought a touch of terror to his heart, even as the loss of his sister brought tears. Therefore, he set Paris the task to travel to Greece with another lord of Troy, Aeneas, find his lost sister Hesione, and bring her home to Troy. Paris bowed before his newly recognized father and prepared to set sail on his quest.

CHAPTER 3

Helen of Sparta

>>>> · <<<<

Tyndareus of Sparta was called the most blessed and pathetic of Greece's kings. The most blessed because his wife had given him four beautiful children, the most wonderful children any man could hope for. The most pathetic because three died tragically young, all but Helen. His wife Leda died of grief, leaving him alone with Helen. While she was beautiful, indeed the most beautiful mortal woman in the world, they said, the law of the land decreed that she could not rule alone once Tyndareus died. So Tyndareus had a problem, for many lords, nobles, and even kings had asked him for Helen's hand in marriage. But such was her beauty that he feared the war would break out depending on whom he chose as her husband. He sought the advice of wily Odysseus, king of Ithaca, and together they hatched a plan. Calling the various suitors together at his palace, he addressed them all:

"Welcome, noble lords of Greece. It does me and my house great honor just to have you standing here, all eager to wed my only daughter and rule Sparta when the fates decide my time is done. I ask only one thing: You shall all swear now, before each other and before the gods, that you shall all honor and protect the marriage of Helen, no matter whom I choose."

Every man was silent a moment, but every man hoped in his heart that he would be chosen. So, every man swore the oath willingly, lest another man should dare to steal Helen away. Tyndareus bowed his head in thanks, his heart finally at peace. He looked around the circle of expectant faces one more time. Some stood out, of course. Mighty Ajax, big as an oak; noble Menelaus, brother of King Agamemnon of Mycenae; Diomedes, swift as his spear. So many good choices for his beloved daughter. Breathing deeply, he raised his chin and said, "Menelaus."

A year had passed since Helen married Menelaus, and at this time, Paris came to Sparta. He and a fellow Trojan lord, Aeneas, had been sent by Priam in a final attempt to seek the return of his long-lost sister, Hesione. She had been taken prisoner from Troy by Herakles and Telemon when Priam was still young, and she, like her brother, was now old. But Priam still hoped the Greeks would allow her to return to her homeland before she died. They faced one problem, however: Telemon had died years before, and his sons: Ajax and Teucer, were rarely at home. Therefore, Paris and Aeneas were chasing around Greece's many isles and cities, trying to find the wandering heroes to lay their father's plea before them.

As it so happened, Menelaus was also not home when the two sons of Troy arrived, weary from many days at sea and tired of their long chase. But Paris knew that no matter if they learned nothing of Ajax and Teucer's whereabouts, it did his city no harm to foster friendships with the Greeks. Troy sat on the Hellespont, a thin strait of water that led to the Black Sea. Thus, good trading relationships with the Greeks were essential. Hitching his best cloak around his shoulders, Paris led Aeneas and a handful of men up through Sparta's streets to the royal palace.

Meanwhile, Queen Helen stared moodily out of the window in the palace of Sparta itself. Her father had died just three months after her marriage to Menelaus, and she suspected now that he had been holding himself to life just long enough to see her married. She knew she was supposed to be grateful to her father for his care, but she wasn't. Menelaus was a great warrior, all sung his praise, and he had good relations with the local lords and kings of Greece, but her marriage to him was hardly a happy one. Menelaus spent much of his time away from the city, riding, hunting, and training up the Spartan army, which, Helen had to admit, had seen better days. When he was at home, he would be drinking, planning, and complaining to Helen that he didn't already have a son and heir.

"Life as a queen is not life as a princess." She reminded herself for about the hundredth time with a sigh. Then a knock at the door arose her from her reverie. "Come in!" She called.

Palastor, the royal advisor, entered. "My lady, a delegation from Troy has arrived. Will you see them?"

Frowning slightly, Helen nodded. She had no choice. Menelaus was not expected back for at least another week, and the law of hospitality demanded to be respectful to her guests. Snapping her fingers at her handmaidens, she prepared quickly and was seated in the great hall before the Trojan princes were announced.

Helen sighed as the doors opened, ready for the usual group of armored, dusty, bearded men, all convinced of their own good looks – whether they had them or not – and determined to drink as much and eat as much as they could before the night was out. Sparta's vineyards and farms were rich and abundant; she had no fears there – but it was rather dull. And then she saw Paris. He was tall, as tall as Menelaus but slighter of build, his hair dark and curly. But his eyes and his smile were what drew her. They just looked so natural, like a man who hadn't spent years hunting or fighting or staring at troop lists and weapon orders. No, Paris looked like a man she could talk to and laugh with. Helen smiled broadly, possibly for the first time she had really smiled since her father had died.

"Come, noble lords of Troy!" She said, rising from her throne. "Come sit by me and eat and drink. When you are rested, you can tell us of your journey and your quest."

Paris could not take his eyes off the queen. He had heard tales during their travels of Helen, but all fell short of the true wonder of this radiant woman standing before them. The gentle softness of her smile, the way her hair fell like a golden waterfall, the sparkles like tiny stars that made her eyes light up. Paris had judged between three goddesses, so one could say he knew something of beauty. While nothing could compare between a mortal woman and an immortal goddess, there was no getting away from the fact that

The Road to War

Helen was the most stunning, glorious, wonderful, charming woman he had ever seen. Even as he stood there, mouth slightly open, words spoken to him back in Troy came back to him, echoing in his ear: "…I will give you the love of the most beautiful woman in the world. She shall be yours, and you shall be happy." He had chosen to give Aphrodite, the goddess of love, the golden apple, and she had promised him the love of the most beautiful woman in the world. All thoughts of returning Hesione to Troy fell away as he looked at Helen. She was his quest now. If he couldn't return to Troy with her, then he wouldn't be returning at all.

The day wore on, with wine and laughter and singing. The Trojans found that they quite liked the Spartans, and the Spartans found that they quite liked the Trojans. Aeneas and Palastor spent much of the evening sharing stories – it seemed that Aeneas' father Anchises had known Palastor when they were young men, and the old Spartan had much to tell the young Trojan of their adventures back then. As the evening drew in and the stars came out, everyone went to bed. Everyone, that is, except for Helen and Paris. Neither seemed to grow tired even as the moon arched high overhead, sending down her soft beams. Needing some fresh air, Helen asked Paris to accompany her out for a walk. They were strolling along at ease when Paris turned to her and asked, "Do you like it here in Sparta?"

"Like it?" She paused. "Yes, I've lived here my whole life. It's my home."

"So, you're happy here?"

She paused again.

"Helen?"

Biting her lip, she turned away, leaning on the wall. "I was, once, when my father was alive. But it's been different since Menelaus."

Paris stepped to her side. "Are you happy here?"

She turned to him, to that wonderful, honest, kind face glimmering in the moonlight. "No, I'm not."

He grasped her hand, his words tumbling out. "Come with me then! Come to Troy!"

For a second, she couldn't breathe. Then they held hands under the moonlight, and they were on a ship headed east the next day.

CHAPTER 4

The Greeks Assemble

Agamemnon and his brother Menelaus could not be happier that day. Menelaus was still growling like an angry bear about what he would do to Paris when he got his hands on him, but the heralds kept coming back with good news. They had called all the great lords and nobles of Greece to bring their warriors. The first, of course, were the suitors of Helen: those lords and kings who had also asked for her hand in marriage and who had sworn the same oath Menelaus had to support whomever her father Tyndareus chose as her husband. They had no choice, as honor was at stake. Mighty Ajax, with his great shield like a tower, had brought 12 ships; Diomedes, a young but experienced commander, had brought 80 ships.

"And more will come, brother!" Smiled Agamemnon as they looked out over the bay from a high tower, looking down at the milling ships below. "Even the winds favor us!" A gentle but consistent breeze was blowing straight towards Aulis, allowing accessible entrance for all incoming ships.

Menelaus grunted. "The suitors will come, of course, or I will speak with them myself. But Troy's walls were built by the gods themselves, they say. We shall need an army greater than Greece has ever seen to take it."

His brother's smile broadened. "Yes, Troy is strong. Its fields are rich. And that is why men will flock to our banner. If not for honor, then for gold and glory!"

Footsteps on the tower's stairs made both turn around. Old Nestor, Agamemnon's advisor, and Calchas, a priest who could read the stars and the signs from the gods, came puffing up.

"My lords," gasped Nestor, sitting on the stairs to rest. "Calchas has had a vision!"

The brothers turned to the thin oracle who bowed.

"Hear these words from the great god Apollo:

Glory and honor and gold and power await at Troy.

But only if the lion of Phthia sails with you."

"The lion of Phthia?" Scoffed Agamemnon. "What does that mean? We aren't a traveling circus!"

Nestor cleared his throat. "My lord, the lion of Phthia isn't a creature; it's a man! We must send for Achilles, son of Peleus, and his Myrmidons!"

Menelaus and Agamemnon both rolled their eyes at each other.

"He's just a kid!" Cried Menelaus.

"He can't be controlled!" Shouted Agamemnon.

"He's the greatest warrior in Greece!" Snapped Nestor, rising to his feet. "We need him; the gods have spoken!"

Agamemnon sighed. "Well, then there's only one man he'll listen to. We must send word to Odysseus of Ithaca."

Odysseus, king of Ithaca, was the happiest he had ever been. He had heard the dark news of war with Troy, but that morning his beloved wife Penelope had given birth to their first child, a boy: Telemachus. But his heart was still troubled even as he stood atop the highest point of Ithaca, showing his kingdom to his son and heir. "This will all be yours one day, Telemachus," he whispered, shielding his son's eyes from the brightness of the dappled waves and the open sky. Looking back at sea, he gasped, "May the gods protect us! That can only be a ship from Mycenae." Holding the now wriggling Telemachus firmly, he half-ran back to his and Penelope's room. Handing her their son, he explained his plan, already well-formed in his mind.

By the time Palamedes, the messenger of Agamemnon, jumped onto Ithaca's harbor, Penelope, holding Telemachus to her chest, was already waiting for him. "My lord?" Penelope said confusedly. "I'm sorry, I do not believe we have been lucky enough to welcome you to Ithaca before. May I take you inside and offer you something to refresh your strength before you tell us your business here?"

Palamedes glared at her for a moment but bowed his head curtly. "I am Palamedes." He paused and then continued stiffly, "Queen Penelope, I am sorry to have to bother you on such a happy day," he gestured to the infant, "but I must speak with Odysseus."

Penelope's eyes filled with tears. "It is a happy day, lord Palamedes, but not for my husband. A sickness has filled his mind. I don't know which god has cursed our island, cruelly so as our son has come to bless it."

"I ask this for the last time," growled Palamedes. "Where is Odysseus?"

Penelope said nothing, only gestured further along the shore.

The golden sand of Ithaca glowed in the mid-morning light, but long, uneven lines covered the beach's gentle smoothness. They could hear a man yelling as they hurried along the coast. Palamedes opened his mouth, surprised at what he saw. Odysseus had hooked a donkey and an ox to a plow. He tried to till the sandy beach, even as the waves lapped at his feet. Palamedes glanced back at Penelope, then again at the madman before him. Eyes narrowed, he seized the infant Telemachus from her, even as she screamed in protest. Laying the crying child on the sand before the plow, Palamedes watched as Odysseus drove the mismatched animals relentlessly forwards.

At the last moment, Odysseus cried aloud and heaved on the reins, causing the exhausted beasts to stop. Running forwards, Odysseus scooped his son from the sand, tears falling down his cheeks. "My boy! My son!" Then he rounded on Palamedes, who stood, hands on hips, smiling triumphantly. "Calm down, Odysseus!" He shouted. "Your plan is uncovered. King Agamemnon calls for you and your warriors. We sail for Phthia and then for Troy!"

Achilles, son of Peleus, was considered the greatest warrior ever by many Greeks. He was very young but had already fought many battles and had come through everyone without a scratch. Some said that his mother, the sea-nymph Thetis, had taken him as a baby and anointed him with ambrosia, the food of the gods, dipped him in waters from the River Styx, which flowed through the Underworld, and then held him over the fire, to make him invulnerable. However, she could not finish the ritual as Peleus had stopped her – not knowing what she was doing to their infant son. Thus, Achilles' only weak spot was his heel because that was where Thetis had held him during the rite.

Thetis, being a nymph, had already heard about the Greek troops' gathering forces and knew they would want her son to go with them. But she knew something else, too: She had heard an oracle foretold that her son would have two choices: either to live long but without glory or to die young and be remembered forever.

"I didn't go through all that trouble getting the water from the River Styx, just for him to die at Troy!" She cried, so one night, she took the teenage Achilles away from Phthia to the nearby city of Skyros. With the king's permission, she hid Achilles among the female servants, forcing him to dress as a girl so that no one would think it was him.

The Road to War

Palamedes and Odysseus arrived at Phthia not long after and were not convinced by Thetis' story that her son had run away. Odysseus sneaked around the palace, questioning the servants. So he learned of Thetis' night-time ride with her son. Guessing that she would not have taken him far, he and Palamedes decided to search the nearby towns and cities.

Coming to Skyros, they questioned the king carefully and could not get any information out of him at all. Disappointed, they turned to leave, at which point Odysseus noticed that one of the servant girls was taller than all the guards. Elbowing Palamedes, he drew his sword and shouted for their own men to seize the servants. There was instant uproar. All the girls ran wildly, screaming for their lives. All but one: the tall servant, Odysseus had noticed, ran forwards, seizing a spear from a surprised guard and charging into the fight.

"Stop, Achilles!" Odysseus shouted, sheathing his sword and holding his hands high. "Stop all of you!" The young man in the dress stared at him, realizing now what had happened. Then his face broke into a wide smile.

"I told mother I wanted to go to Troy." He pulled off the dark wig that had covered his blond curls. "I guess I have no choice now but to do what you ask?"

Palamedes shouldered his way over and clapped Achilles on the shoulder. "That's right! No choice at all. Sad for you: all that glory, honor, and gold are waiting at Troy."

"Yes," said Odysseus quietly to himself as he turned away. "And how do we get it? By traveling halfway around the world and fighting a war." He shook his head. "I hope it's worth it."

CHAPTER 5

The Greeks sail for Troy.

All the Greeks were assembled at Aulis. The camp stretched far and wide around the small port city. Nestor had counted all the ships and taken the lists from all the captains and lords and kings. Over 1,000 ships were docked in the bay at Aulis, and well over 100,000 soldiers stood ready to sail to Troy. There was, however, one problem: The gentle breeze that had guided all those ships safely into Aulis had gotten stronger. Now tall waves pounded the edges of the bay and worried the captains, lest their ships should bash into each other. No vessel could now leave Aulis without great effort; indeed, no ship could sail to Troy.

Agamemnon paced the tower with his closest advisors: Menelaus, Nestor, Odysseus, and Calchas.

"We've been here for weeks!" Raged the king of Mycenae, clenching his fists and grinding his teeth. "How long can this wind last?"

The other lords looked at each other and just shrugged.

"We should ask the gods again to change the winds' direction." Said Nestor.

Odysseus shook his head. "The gods are the cause of this wind – there can't be another reason for it constantly blowing this way. We need to find out which one it is and do something to make them change their mind."

Agamemnon agreed. "This can't go on. Keeping soldiers happy is hard enough. There's actual fighting to do, but keeping this lot," he jerked his thumb over his shoulder at the vast fields of tents stretching into the distance, "happy and quiet just sitting on their hands waiting for the wind to change is going to be impossible. They'll start fighting amongst themselves soon."

"And," said Menelaus, "the lesser lords, those who were not suitors for Helen, who are only here for gold and glory, will also get bored of waiting soon and leave!"

Therefore, they sent Calchas to discover which god and sacrifice were needed to change the winds' direction before it was too late. He came back three days later, but his news was not what they had hoped. It seemed that, many years ago, Agamemnon had hunted and killed a deer that was sacred to Artemis, goddess of the moon. Although he had no idea at the time, he had angered the goddess, and now she was sending these winds to stop the Greek fleet from sailing to Troy. When asked what could be done to make the goddess happy, Calchas was, at first, unwilling to say anything more. He seemed terrified of what he had learned.

"I'll speak, King Agamemnon," he trembled, "only if you give me your solemn oath that no harm shall come to me, no matter what happens."

Frowning, Agamemnon looked at his council of lords, all looked just as confused as he did, but they all shrugged and nodded. Once Agamemnon had sworn the oath, Calchas stepped forward and explained what would appease the goddess.

"Artemis does not require bulls, horses, deer, or even a bear sacrificed to her. She's the goddess of the hunt as well as the moon. No creature can outrun her hounds or escape her arrows. What the goddess desires is this, my lord Agamemnon: You must sacrifice your eldest daughter, Iphigenia."

There was a stunned silence, during which Agamemnon seemed to wilt like a flower in autumn that can feel the winter coming. He shook his head wordlessly, his eyes wide and staring. Nestor stepped forwards carefully. "My lord, perhaps you need some time to take this news in properly?" Agamemnon didn't say a word but left the room immediately. The other kings looked at each other, then Odysseus said, "It's a terrible thing to ask any man, but what choice is there?"

The evening had drawn in when Menelaus, accompanied by Nestor, banged on his brother's door. There was a moment's silence before they called inside. Agamemnon sat with his head in his hands; his eyes were very bloodshot. They glanced at each other, and then Nestor spoke. "My king, the council of lords has voted, and all agree that Iphigenia must die. You have no choice but to do what you must for your people."

Nestor stepped forward. "We have written a letter from you to your wife, Clytemnestra. She will bring Iphigenia here, believing that she is to be betrothed to Achilles before we set sail."

Nestor continued. "Once they arrive, Odysseus will distract the queen, and we will take the girl aside and do what must be done."

Agamemnon raised his head to look at the old man. There was a steely look in his eye he had rarely seen there before. Hands shaking, Agamemnon took the letter and signed it.

When Clytemnestra and Iphigenia arrived, the clouds seemed to be darkening with approaching storms. Odysseus showed Clytemnestra around the harbor while Agamemnon and Nestor took Iphigenia to meet Achilles for their first meeting. The formal betrothal ceremony would take place that evening, he said. Clytemnestra had also wanted to meet Achilles, but Nestor had persuaded her not to, saying, "let the girl enjoy this moment for herself, my queen." Then he and Agamemnon led the excited girl away.

"Where are we going, father?" Asked Iphigenia, smiling sweetly up at him. It broke his heart to see her so happy, so innocent. He clenched his teeth into a smile and said, "You'll see soon enough, my dearest child." Nestor had already had everything prepared; a great pile of wood stood in a forest clearing outside of Aulis, a single, colossal log set upright in the center. To this, they tied Iphigenia, who was crying with terror. "What are you doing, father?" She wailed. Tears were rolling down Agamemnon's cheeks as he took the burning torch from Nestor and raised his eyes to the sky. "Great goddess Artemis, hear my prayer and accept this sacrifice! I am sorry for my insult to you." His voice choked in his throat as he continued. "Take my daughter!" And he set the wood on fire, even as Iphigenia screamed.

Then another voice echoed down from the trees. "I hear you, king of Mycenae." Staring round in sudden terror, Agamemnon could see the shadowy forms of wolves and bears, deer and foxes. Then a bright light shone through the branches. Holding his hands up before his eyes, Agamemnon squinted through his fingers and saw a woman stepping onto the burning logs. With a single slice of her hunting knife, she cut the ropes binding his daughter and lifted her lightly down from the fire. The goddess glanced at Agamemnon and said, "Your daughter is now mine. She shall serve me forever as one of my hunters." Then the light shone still brighter, so bright that he could not look. When he opened his eyes again, he could not see anything except the trees, the fire, and Nestor staring at him open-mouthed.

"Did that just happen?" Asked the old man breathlessly. "What does this mean?"

The king shrugged his shoulders, murmuring, "I don't know. I can only hope that the goddess takes care of

Iphigenia and allows us to leave for Troy." He turned away from the fire, heading back to Aulis, his shoulders drooping, his face downcast, and his heart heavy.

Agamemnon sat alone on the docks, watching the ships bob up and down, listening to the scream of the gulls, still trying to work out if what he had just seen had been real or not. Then his heart tensed as he sensed a change in the air. The rustling of the trees was different somehow. Looking up, he saw the storm clouds were now chasing away from Aulis again, back out to sea. The sacrifice or whatever had happened, had worked. The goddess was satisfied. The winds had changed. Agamemnon and his fleet of 1,000 ships would be going to war.

The next day, even as Agamemnon reveled in the singing of happy men loading their ships, one voice carried towards him on the breeze. His wife, Clytemnestra, was in mourning and wouldn't talk to anyone. He had not expected her to believe that a goddess had spirited Iphigenia away at the last moment. No words seemed enough to express her rage, hurt, and loss. He understood; he had betrayed her and his daughter, but that was his burden to bear. He had a greater task ahead of him now, and he would not falter. He had sworn that they would take Troy, whatever the cost. As he stood on the deck of his flagship, he wondered if he should have at least tried to say goodbye to Clytemnestra but shook the thought away. He would return in a few months, his ships laden with gold and slaves and tales of glory. In the meantime, she would have calmed down and come to understand why he had done what he did. Raising his arm to signal to the nearest ships, Agamemnon cried aloud to the men and to all who could hear, "We sail! We sail for Troy! We shall not return without glory and gold, more than any of us can carry!" A cheer went up as the mainsail was raised. It billowed in the wind, and with a lurch that quickened Agamemnon's heart, they were off.

Part II

The Trojan War

The Trojan War

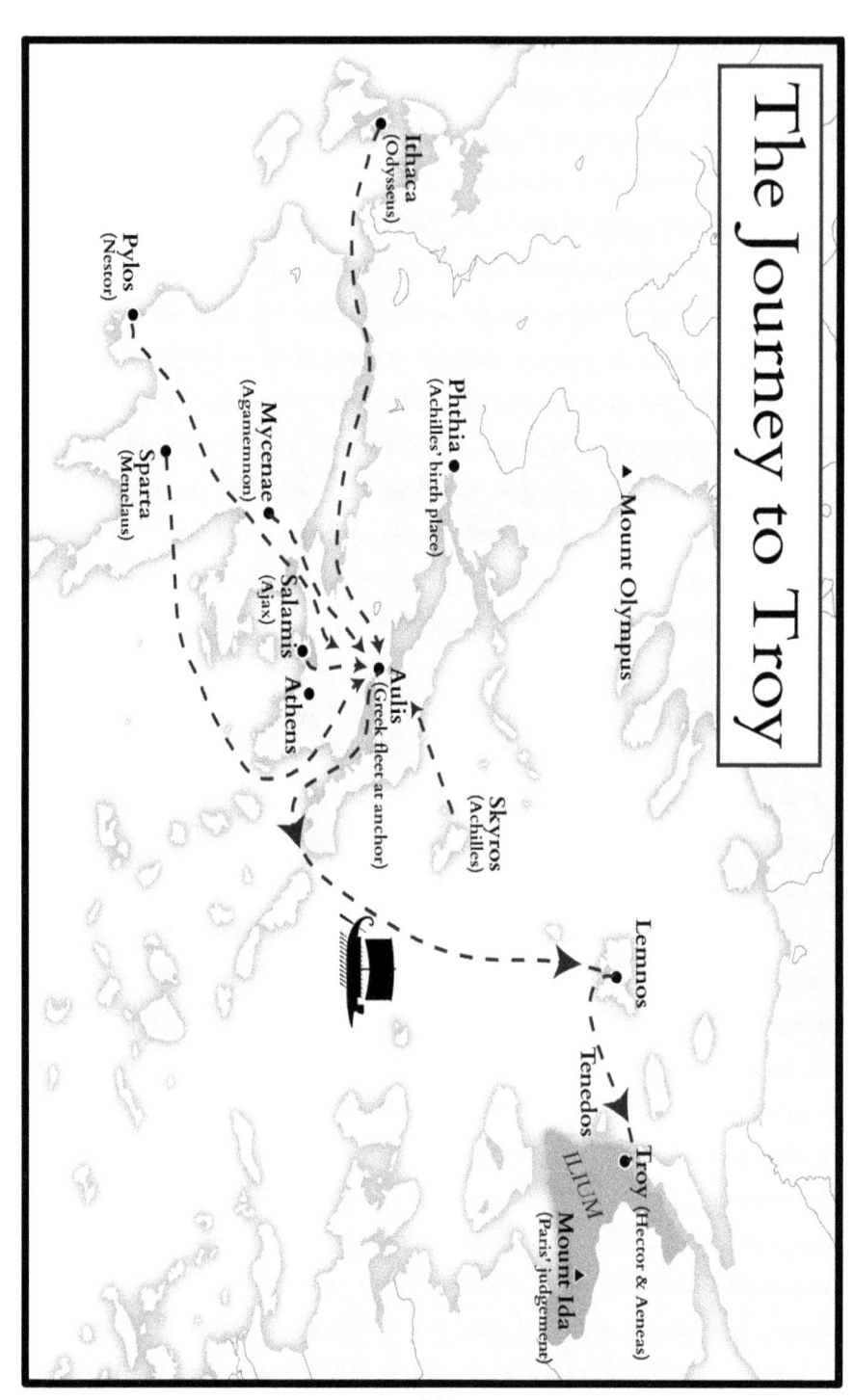

The Journey to Troy

CHAPTER 1

An Archer, a Prophecy, and a Curse

⋙ · ⋘

The voyage from Aulis to Troy was a long and difficult one. There was a little open sea between the two. The fleet had to navigate between the many islands of Greece. Anchoring the ships at Lemnos, Agamemnon called a council to discuss the final plans for storming the beaches at Ilium, the state of Troy. But on arrival at his tent, the lords were met by a genuinely terrible smell. Covering their mouths and noses, they searched for the source. Outside the tent sat Philoctetes, the last surviving companion of the great hero Herakles. He had been chosen to light the funeral pyre and honored with the gift of Herakles' bow. Now, he sat outside Agamemnon's tent, his face twisted with pain.

The source of the smell was not hard to find. Philoctetes' foot was swollen, green, and covered in angry boils. "I stepped off the ship and into the bushes to find my men something to eat." Explained to the other lords, none of whom wanted to step too close. "And then I got this massive pain in my foot. A snake bit me, I think."

"Can none of the healers help?" Asked Diomedes, looking a little green himself because of the smell. The archer shook his head. "They've tried, but they're clueless. I've asked Calchas if he can come up with a remedy or tell me what god I need to kill a chicken for or whatever."

Agamemnon pushed through the tent flaps, wrinkling his nose at the disgusting stench, just as Calchas, the priest, arrived. Taking Agamemnon and Odysseus aside, Calchas whispered. "I've never seen such a wound before, my lords. From what I can tell, this is a curse, not a bite."

Agamemnon's eyes raised. "A curse?" He looked over his shoulder quickly at Philoctetes. "I don't like the man much, but what can he possibly have done to deserve this?" Calchas shrugged. "I haven't been able to discover that, my king."

Odysseus cut in. "This is hardly a good omen. We haven't even got to Troy, and already we've got soldiers being cursed by unknown gods who won't reveal their intentions. My lord," he touched Agamemnon on the arm. "You have already given up so much for this expedition. Let's not risk it all due to one man. Leave Philoctetes here, and we sail on to Troy."

"Oi! I heard that!" Shouted Philoctetes, struggling to his feet and limping over. "You think you can leave me behind?! Well, I've got news for you, Odysseus – you need me! There's a prophecy that says Troy will only fall to an army bearing the arms of Herakles. Well," he gestured to his bow. "I've got the bow of Herakles, and no one's taking it from me. So, there's no leaving me behind!"

Calchas looked puzzled. "I've never heard of such a prophecy, my friend. Are you sure?"

"Positive!" Backed the archer. "Now go make yourself useful and mix me up a potion to cure this damn foot." He limped off.

That evening, Odysseus and Diomedes entered the tent of Philoctetes, eyes watering due to the stench that filled the room. "Calchas sent us with this." Murmured Diomedes, averting his eyes from the disgusting foot and placing a cup of potion by Philoctetes's chair. "Thank you." Snapped the sick man, and he downed the cup in two gulps. "Now, get out; I can't imagine you want to stay here much," he yawned, "ahem, longer." His eyes began to droop, and then a fierce look of suspicion shot over his face. "What was that..?" He tried to rise, but then his head fell onto his chest, and he began snoring.

Odysseus grinned. "I told you it would work. Now let's grab the bow and get to the ships." He reached forward to grab the weapon, but Diomedes held him back, shaking his head.

"What's your problem?" Asked Odysseus angrily.

"It's bad enough that we're leaving him behind on this island." Replied Diomedes firmly. "We will not take his weapon – given to him by Herakles himself. We will not sink to such dishonor!"

"You know what he said: we need the bow to take Troy!"

Diomedes rolled his eyes. "Oh, come on. Philoctetes is a great archer and a better liar. Calchas hasn't heard of any such oracle, and I trust Calchas over him any day."

"Fine." Growled Odysseus. "Let's get going. Who knows when he'll wake up."

A few days later, when the fleet was nearly at Troy, Odysseus lay asleep in his ship, and a dream came to him: His ship was fast approaching the shores of Ilium, and he could see the waves breaking on the shore. They were finally there! As though floating above like a ghost, he watched himself readying his shield and spear and saw the spray fly up as the solid Odysseus leaped into the shallow water. He was the first Greek to set foot on Trojan soil! The "spirit-Odysseus" watched Odysseus on the ground run forwards, laughing and shouting for all to follow him. Then an arrow flew out of nowhere, catching the hero in the chest. He crashed to the ground, even as the floating Odysseus yelled and tried to pull the arrow's shaft out, invisible fingers passing through the wood like smoke.

Odysseus woke with a start, cold sweat pouring down his face. Had he just seen his own death? A shiver ran down his spine. He wasn't a priest; he had no such skills. Never in his life had he received such visions. Was it a message? A warning from the gods? He tossed and turned for the rest of the night, considering every possibility. The next morning the lookout at the top of the mast cried, "Land ahead! It's Troy!" Odysseus felt a lump in his throat like he had swallowed a stone. He readied his armor carefully, strapping it tightly. Might this be my last day? He wondered.

In no time at all, the ship was rocking up and down as they neared the shore. "Protesilaus!" Called Odysseus. "Come with me! I need a good man at my back as we storm the beach. They are bound to have seen our coming, and we must be ready for a strong defense."

Protesilaus, a young man whose beard was coming through, looked excited as he took his place by his king at the front of the ship. As they heard wood grating on the sand and felt the ship heave to a stop, Odysseus leaped up to the front of the boat. "Come, men! Glory and honor await us just over there!" He gestured with his shield arm, and with a splash, his great shield came loose and dropped into the water. Smiling ruefully, he turned to his men. "My shield is braver than me!" Everyone laughed as Odysseus turned and jumped down, landing square on his shield which lay just beneath the water. "Come, Protesilaus! Cover me while I get my shield out of the sand!" He ordered.

Another splash as the young soldier leaped down obediently and raised his shield. "Go on!" called Odysseus. "Push forwards. It's stuck! Kill a Trojan for me!" Protesilaus smiled over his shoulder and cried aloud, "For Greece and glory!" Odysseus paused, taking care not to step off his shield as he watched the man charge forwards through the surf, more of his comrades now splashing down to follow him. There was a sudden cry, and he saw a body fall, an arrow sticking out of its chest. No longer smiling, he retrieved his shield and strode forwards, holding it high to protect himself from further arrows.

Protesilaus' young face still held that proud, excited expression, even as he lay dead on the sands of Ilium. Odysseus knelt by the body and said a silent prayer to his spirit. "I'm sorry, Protesilaus. I'm sorry you did not get to kill your first Trojan. You were the first to step on Trojan soil, so you were the first to fall, and I have more to do in this life. I shall make sure you are buried properly and will send a chest of gold home to Ithaca for your parents."

With that, he rose and drew his sword. "Forth, comrades!" He cried. "One of us has fallen, but 100,000 follow us! Let us bring fire and sword, blood and slaughter to the land of Troy!"

As he stepped past the body of his fallen comrade, there was no way that Odysseus could know that Troy would not fall so easily. Zeus looked down at him from Mount Olympus and frowned. "These mortals think that fate can be changed so easily." He snorted. "This is the last great act in the age of heroes, and it will not pass by lightly. I foresee many difficult years ahead for Trojan and Greek alike."

CHAPTER 2

Agamemnon dishonors Achilles

》》》· ·《《《

The war at Troy had waged on for nine years. Nine, long, painful years. The Greeks had won many early victories and had taken war across the land of Ilium. They attacked and captured towns, they enslaved hundreds, even thousands of the people living around Troy. There were many battles. Some of the Greeks won; some of the Trojans won. But the walls of Troy still stood, as high and as impassable as when Herakles had stood at their base and demanded his prize, all those years ago. The Trojans were said to have the greatest archers in the world, and certainly, few if any Greeks had made it even within a stone's throw of the walls. When the Trojans sallied out to meet the Greeks in open battle, they were always led by Hector, the eldest son of Priam, and he seemed to have no rival.

In all the years at Troy, however, Achilles had never set a blade against Hector. Some said that it was just sheer luck, others said that the gods themselves had found a way to keep these two mighty heroes apart. Achilles himself had grown into a great warrior and leader of men. His youthful excitement for battle had been replaced by a hard weariness, although he still loved gold as much as ever. No matter the number of victories, however, no Greek could deny that they were in a terrible stalemate. All had thought that Troy would have fallen within a matter of months, but this war seemed to have no end.

In the midst of all this horror and constant battle, came Chryses, high priest of Apollo. He came alone without fear, for his position with the god protected him, and he was also well-known for his peaceful, trustworthy nature. He brought two donkeys with him, each carrying a heavy chest, full of gold. At the entrance to the Greek camp, he begged a meeting with Agamemnon, for his daughter, Chryseis, had been captured some days before by the Greeks and he hoped he could barter her safe return. But Agamemnon would not listen to the priest's pleas. Chryseis was beautiful, and the king of Mycenae already had plenty of gold, his allotted share from all the plunder of Ilium. He spat in the priest's face and kicked him out of his tent, laughing all the while.

The gods themselves were watching this, and Apollo, enraged at the insult to his priest, barely waited for the man's prayers of revenge before he leaped down from Olympus, his bow in hand, arrows clattering furiously in the quiver on his back. He settled on Mount Ida, overlooking the Greek camp, and selected an arrow. He whispered dark words of sickness and death over the arrow, nocked it to the bowstring, and took careful aim. The arrow flew through the air as silent as breath, striking a Greek soldier in the neck. He did not fall to the ground, not noticing the arrow as it dissolved like smoke as soon as he raised his hand to his throat. He gave a single cough and then went on about his work. Arrow after arrow fell into the Greek camp, and soon there were many soldiers coughing all around. But this was no simple illness, Apollo had sent a plague to the Greek camp, and before the sun had risen twice more, men were dying.

"As if we did not have enough to worry about!" Grumbled Odysseus in the council of lords a few days later. "Hector and his men just need to sit on the walls and watch us die. This war will be over before another month is out!"

"Calm yourself, friend Odysseus." sighed Nestor, bent with age as he sat to the left of Agamemnon. He had been old before coming to Troy, and nine years of worry had aged him even more. "I'm sure that Calchas will return soon with the answer, he has never failed us yet."

"I can't wait." Snapped Odysseus, seating himself again as the tent flap opened and the priest Calchas was brought quickly inside. He looked nervously at the lords and began,

"My lords, I have discovered the source of this plague, but before I speak, I would ask that you all swear to protect me, in case my words anger one of you."

Achilles rolled his eyes. "Come on, Calchas. We've been here nine long years. Your oracles have not always been welcome, but they have never been wrong. Trust us as we trust you. If you are so scared I will swear to guard you from any here, even high king Agamemnon himself if needs be. Now spit it out!"

Calchas swallowed, and then spoke quickly. "Thank you, lord Achilles. The plague is sent by Apollo, as might be expected, him being the god of such things. But the reason is actually quite simple: The god is angry over the treatment of his priest, Chryses. Our lord and high king Agamemnon insulted him, refused his ransom for his daughter, and threw him out of the camp. The girl must be returned as soon as possible, without ransom. Then Apollo will end the plague."

All eyes turned to Agamemnon, who sighed and rose. Calchas backed away. "Don't be afraid, Calchas. As Achilles said, your oracles are not always welcome, but you are right. I have offended Apollo, I must set this right. I will return the girl Chryseis, but…"

"What, but?!" Interjected Achilles, his temper suddenly rising, though he had no idea why. "That's it! Just give the girl back, no questions asked, and our men stop dying. What's there to say "but" about?"

Agamemnon's eyes narrowed. "Do not test me, boy. I will not go without compensation. Chryses had offered a rich reward for his daughter, Chryseis, but I am supposed to go without this now. That will not do. My honor and rights as high king over all of you demand that I be treated with respect. If I do not have a prize like Chryseis, then I must have another."

"Where from?!" Achilles shouted, spreading his arms wide and looking around the tent in mock astonishment. "I have personally captured twelve cities across Ilium since we got here, there are no other places to capture within a week's march of Troy, save Troy itself. Unless someone is hiding a pretty girl somewhere, we have nothing more to give you. Every time we capture slaves or seize gold; the spoils are divided among us. You always take your share, more than your fair share, some might say, and what have you done to deserve it?"

Agamemnon rose to face the young warrior. "I am warning you boy, one more word and you'll pay dearly. As it is, I think I will just take your prize instead. What was her name, Briseis? A pretty thing, I seem to remember, not as pretty as Chryseis but she will do."

There was silence in the tent. Odysseus could hear his own heart beating.

"You sack of wine!" Growled Achilles. "You dare dishonor me on top of your insult to the god?! My hands have killed more in a day in Ilium than yours have in a lifetime. It is my victories that have kept Hector at bay, my glory that makes the men sing in the evening. Do this and I will fight no longer. My men and I will stay by our ship and let's see how long it is before Hector himself stands in this tent and demands more than you can give."

Agamemnon raised an eyebrow. "Any yet in nine years you have never once managed to kill Hector? You must keep missing each other on the battlefield, or perhaps you are just afraid to face him."

It took Ajax and Odysseus together to restrain Achilles and push him away from Agamemnon.

"I swear that before my time is done, I will have my revenge!" Shouted Achilles, before he allowed the two heroes to steer him out of the tent.

"Right!" smiled Agamemnon, unconcerned. "Diomedes, when Odysseus returns, have him get the girl ready for transport to her father. I think it is also a good idea to sacrifice something to Apollo himself, just to make sure. Odysseus will know what to do. Then have one of my heralds go fetch Briseis from Achilles' tent."

It was evening by the time Chryseis opened the door to her father's house and was received with welcome thanks by Chryses. Meanwhile, Odysseus was administering the sacrifice of no less than one hundred bulls to Apollo. Satisfied, the god unstrung his bow and left Mount Ida for Olympus again. Within days the plague had vanished from the camp and men thanked the gods and king Agamemnon for rescuing them from their suffering. Achilles sat in his tent, angrily sharpening his sword for the tenth time, muttering dark words as he stared into the fire, thinking of ways he could get revenge on Agamemnon.

CHAPTER 3

The Fight between Menelaus and Paris

>>>> · <<<<

If Achilles had thought his threat would bring Agamemnon sleepless nights, he was mistaken. The Greek leader had fallen swiftly asleep once the council of lords was over. That night, he dreamed that the sky above Mount Ida seemed to glow, the clouds rolled away and a great voice echoed down. "Agamemnon, wake! Wake and raise your men and your banners! Glory awaits at the gates of Troy!" Then the dream faded, and Agamemnon woke, his eyes wide and his heart racing. For nine long years, they had done everything they could to end the stalemate. Now he had a sign from Zeus himself, telling him that victory was at hand!

"This will show, Achilles." He grinned as he strapped his amour on. "We don't need him while the gods themselves favor us!"

He marched around the camp, calling the heralds to sound the trumpets and bringing his council together.

Climbing a great rock that stood in the middle of the camp, he addressed the men, some still rubbing the sleep from their eyes. "My friends and comrades!" He called. "Clear your eyes and sharpen your swords! Zeus himself came to me in a dream last night, promising glory at Troy. I know we have had many false starts and empty victories these past nine years, but don't let that hold you back today. To victory!"

The cheers of the soldiers were still ringing in his ears as Agamemnon urged the horses of his chariot forwards. To his right, Menelaus drove his chariot, and to his left, Odysseus. Behind them he could feel as much as hear the pounding of thousands upon thousands of feet, marching toward Troy. Ahead, he could see a flurry of dust and sand rising in the air, meaning that the Trojans were also leading their army out to face them. His heart pounded a little faster. Could this be the day to end the war?

The open plain before Troy was empty and flat. Agamemnon had lost count of the battles and smaller fights that had taken place on this ground. As they drew nearer, he could see three men riding out to meet them. Raising his hand to halt the army, he signaled that Menelaus and Odysseus should join him in the parlay. He soon recognized the three princes of Troy: Hector, eldest son of Priam and their greatest warrior; Aeneas, son of Anchises and cousin to Hector; and Paris. Agamemnon spat over the side of his chariot when his eyes met those of the young prince. This boy had stolen his Menelaus' wife, Helen, nine years ago, and caused this whole, horrible war.

"King Agamemnon," began Hector. "Once again you bring your army to darken the doorstep of our great city. When will you learn that there is no taking Troy?"

Agamemnon's eyes narrowed. "If there was no taking Troy, why are you here? Why not hide behind your walls as you so often have done?"

Hector raised his chin. "To offer you an end to this war. Too many men have died already. We want to go on with our lives without your killing our people, raiding our farms, and attacking our towns. My brother Paris has a proposal."

The young prince was trembling slightly as he stepped forward, but he looked at each of the Greek lords in the eye as he spoke. "Lord Menelaus, nine years ago Helen chose to come with me to Troy. I did not steal her away and yet still you stay here in the fruitless hope that she will come back to you. I propose a fight, just you and me. If I win, the Greek army will leave Ilium, never to return. If you win, Helen will return with you, and this war will still be over. You can keep all the treasure you have plundered from our land but leave us in peace at last."

Menelaus snarled, "It has taken you nine years to grow enough of a beard to step out from behind your walls, from behind your brother, and face me?" He turned to his brother and Odysseus and whispered. "Let's just kill the three of them here and now."

Odysseus did his best to hide his shock. "We are here under a banner of truce, Menelaus! Have you no honor?

The Trojan War

Besides, the challenge has been laid down – you must fight him. You could end this war in five minutes and then we can all go home. Think of the men, they have had enough!"

Agamemnon agreed. He would rather go home with the plunder of Troy itself in his ship, but enough was enough. Menelaus smiled grimly as he turned back to Paris. "So be it, prince of Troy. We shall fight under the terms you have laid out. Taking their spears, Odysseus and Aeneas marked a large square in the earth. Planting a spear at each corner, the four observers stepped away and announced, "The challenge has been accepted. The square has been made. Let no one interfere!" None of the men present realized it, but the gods themselves were watching this duel. High up on Mount Olympus, Aphrodite, goddess of love, sat with her hands to her mouth, desperately worried for Paris. Meanwhile, Athene, the goddess of war, and Hera, the queen of the gods, looked on with grim smiles. "There is no way Paris can defeat Menelaus!" Whispered Athene to Hera.

Down on the plains of Troy, Paris was charging at Menelaus. Bronze rang against bronze as his spear clashed against Menelaus' wide shield. Paris barely had time to duck as the counterattack swept over his head. Shoving his own shield into Menelaus', he tried to push the bigger man back, but Menelaus was laughing. With a great heave, he sent Paris flying and then hurled his spear. Somehow, Paris managed to block the blow, but the spear blade went straight through his shield. Dropping the now useless shield, Paris took his spear in both hands and lunged again and again at Menelaus, who batted each attack aside with ease. Drawing his bright sword, Menelaus parried Paris' next thrust and brought his blade smashing down on the prince's helmet. There was a ringing crash as the sword shattered on impact, but Paris fell to the ground, dazed. His spear rolled away from his hand. Growling, Menelaus seized Paris by the plume of his helmet and began dragging him away toward the Greek army.

Aphrodite had had enough. Swift as thought, she dove down from Olympus and cut the strap of Paris' helmet, freeing him. Then she summoned a mist that enveloped him, hiding him from mortal eyes. Without a word, she carried him back to Troy, laid him in his bed, and then, disguised as a servant girl, went to find Helen. "My lady!" Aphrodite cried. "Lord Paris is in his room and needs your help."

Helen sighed. "Paris has gone to face Menelaus. He has finally realized what honor is, but there is no chance of Paris defeating my husband. If he is here, then he must have run away, and my shame is greater as a result."

Aphrodite's eyes narrowed. "I promised you to Paris, Helen, and I keep my promises. It was not his day to die." And she waved her staff at Helen, causing her to remember the sad life she had had while living with Menelaus, and recalling all the good times she had enjoyed with Paris. "Go to him now!" She commanded. Helen, as if in a daze, nodded and went silently to Paris' room.

Meanwhile, up on Mount Olympus, Athene and Hera were seething with rage over Aphrodite's interference. "We shall see about this!" snarled Athene. She disguised herself as a Trojan soldier and leaped down from Olympus, landing in the Trojan ranks. There she found an archer and said to him. "Friend. I'm afraid for Prince Hector. Menelaus looks like he's going to turn on him and break the sacred truce! Quick! Stop him!" As though in a trance, the archer put an arrow to the bowstring without a word and, taking aim, fired.

Menelaus was yelling about dishonor and demanding a re-match when the arrow flew out of the Trojan ranks and pierced his armor, just above the hip. Roaring with pain and rage, he pointed at Hector and cried. "What treachery is this? You break a sacred banner of truce?"

Hector tried to explain that he had given no such orders, but it was too late. The three Greek heroes were already running back to their army, giving orders to prepare to attack. Hector turned to Aeneas as they returned to their army, resigned to yet another battle, another day of lives lost. "It seems the gods themselves want this war to continue, Aeneas. When will they be satisfied?"

Aeneas readied his shield and spear and shook his head sadly. He had no answer either.

CHAPTER 4

The Duels of Hector

>>>> · <<<<

Even as Helen went to Paris' room, the two armies were marching to meet each other on the wide plain before the walls of Troy. Ordering his men to overlap their shields and stand firm, Hector took his place in the front rank. Behind him, he could hear Aeneas ordering the archers to fire, and he raised his own shield to protect against the Greek's answering volley of arrows. And then came the rending, screaming, frightening chaos of battle. Spears and swords pounded against his shield, and his own spear drew back and forth, back and forth as he attacked and countered and killed. Up ahead he could hear a roaring as though a bear had been unleashed on the battlefield. Running forwards, he saw many Trojan soldiers already lying dead. Before he towered a huge Greek warrior. His shield was near twice the size of a normal man's and if Hector had stood next to him, his forehead would only have reached the man's collarbone. Fearing that Herakles himself had returned from the dead, Hector nevertheless readied himself behind his shield. Then the man turned, hurling a Trojan bodily from him and Hector recognized

Ajax. They had never crossed swords, but he had heard of the man's prowess.

"It's time for my family to regain some honor!" He said to himself and with a great cry he charged at Ajax. The collision of these two heroes was like two waves from rival storms smashing together in the midst of the sea. Ajax bellowed his war cry as he recognized the prince of Troy and brought his spear whipping around to knock Hector off his feet. A clang of bronze resounded as the spear glanced harmlessly off Hector's shield and then Ajax was pressed back, having to bring his own huge shield forth to guard against the Trojan's brutal onslaught.

Even as two bulls who meet on Mount Ida charge at each other, lock horns, and wrestle, both intent on bringing the other to their knees, so fought Hector and Ajax. Ajax was the taller, the stronger, with broader shoulders and huge hands. But Hector fought with a ferocity that scared many who saw it. His sword was the faster, his lunge the longer. Neither man would back down, however. The sun rose in the sky and began to track down into the west again, and still, these two heroes fought. Many men on both sides had seen this epic contest taking place, and soon a great ring of watchers, Trojan and Greek alike, stood around, watching these two heroes slug it out, untiring.

Raising a great rock in his hands, Ajax hurled it at Hector. It struck the center of his shield, sending a great gong-like note up into the sky, making all who stood around cover their ears at the noise. Both men were breathing hard as the sun dipped behind Mount Ida, casting a bloody light over the plain. Regardless, they charged again. As he raised his sword to strike, Hector slipped and felt Ajax's own blade slide up his arm, cutting him just below the shoulder. With a gasp of pain, he stepped back, but the cut didn't seem to be deep. The sight of his own blood brought up, from where he did not know, a shaky laugh. He could not stop laughing even as he dropped to his knees, exhausted. But his voice was not the only one to make the plains ring with mirth. Ajax was leaning on his great shield, his sides shaking and his eyes watering.

"The sun sets on our contest, son of Priam." Grinned Ajax. "And finally, one of us sheds a single drop of blood!"

Hector smiled back. "Like this war, I fear this fight will never end!"

"Me too!" guffawed the great warrior. Sticking his sword into the ground, Ajax offered Hector a huge hand. "Shall we call it quits for today?"

Accepting the offered hand, Hector rose to his feet and looked round at the circle of onlookers. "Here." He offered Ajax his sword. "A gift for you, mighty Ajax."

Ajax took the weapon and bowed his thanks. Unstrapping the great belt that hung about his waist, he handed it to Hector. It was a thing of beauty, decorated with gold and silver with the image of a running horse on the buckle. Shaking hands, the two of them turned away. "Bear our fallen comrades back to the ships!" Called Ajax. "Enough blood has been spilled this day."

Weeks had passed since Achilles' argument with Agamemnon, and the young lord's mood was as dark as ever. Sometimes he stormed around his tent, shouting about dishonor and revenge, other times he would just sit moping by the fire, trying to strum a harp or read. But always the distant sounds of battle, of men dying, of triumphant cries and songs of glory being wafted into his tent on the breeze riled his temper again. His close friend, Patroclus, visited him every day, patiently listening to his friend ranting about Agamemnon for the hundredth time.

As the days wore on, however, Patroclus grew more miserable as he saw more and more soldiers returning injured or dead. As great as Ajax and Diomedes and all the other heroes were, they could not stem the tide of the great heroes of Troy: Hector, Aeneas, and Sarpedon to name but three. Worse still, the morale in the camp lowered with each passing day. Barely a man could keep the hopelessness out of his voice. This war had gone on for nine years and seemed to be without end. Patroclus understood his friend's point of view, but at the same time, the men needed Achilles. He was like a banner for them, fearless and strong. So, one day, Patroclus decided to do something.

Sneaking into Achilles' tent early one morning, he strapped on the hero's armor, pulled the helmet down low, took up the great ash spear and the broad shield, and sneaked out into the camp. As he ran past, soldiers called to each other, their voices bright and excited: "Achilles is back! Achilles is going to battle again!" The helmet hid Patroclus' face and no one realized who he was. Soon the army was behind him, and he led them out into the plains of Ilium. Such was the excitement in the army, that they blew the trumpets as though a full assault on Troy was coming. Patroclus' heart was in his mouth; this was what the men needed! He wasn't Achilles, but he was doing what Achilles should have done. Such was the men's mood, that they were singing already about smashing Troy to the ground.

As they neared the city, Patroclus could see the Trojans swarming out of their gates to meet them. "I can do this!" He told himself and he raised his spear, causing the men to cheer and shout with glee. Then the armies met with a crash of sword on shield, spear on the helm, and Patroclus was lost in the chaos of battle. Trojans, seeing the armor of Achilles, fled before him and he chased them, laughing, right to the gates of Troy. But then the Trojans themselves were cheering. Patroclus turned to see why and felt his heart sink into his stomach. Hector was bearing down on him like a wolf who has seen a young sheep in the meadow. Tightening his grip on the spear, Patroclus charged, but he was not Achilles. The spear now felt heavy in his hand, the shield was a great weight on his arm. With frightening speed, Hector forced him back and back, away from the gates of Troy.

Odysseus had heard the cries of the men as they excitedly followed Achilles. Barely allowing himself to believe it, he had followed as well, scarcely able to keep up with the furious pace set by the younger hero. Never had he seen the men so alive, so ready to fight. But as he came to the gates of Troy, a terrible sight met his eyes. Achilles and Hector were already fighting, and the Trojan was driving the Greeks back with astonishing ease. As if in slow-motion, Odysseus watched as Achilles fell to the ground, and saw the helmet fall from his head. He was too far away to help and so all he could do was watch hopelessly as Hector brought his spear slicing down. No soldier moved. All were staring at the scene unfolding before them. Odysseus ran up even as Hector roared his triumph. Sinking to his knees, Odysseus stared open-mouthed at the dead hero before him. Hector's pitiless eyes fell on him. "You have come to see my great victory, Odysseus!" he roared. "I have killed Achilles!"

Odysseus shook his head.

"You haven't. This is Patroclus, a friend of Achilles. He must have stolen his armor."

Hector stared at him, stunned. "Is this some trick?"

"No. No trick, son of Priam. Take his armor – it's yours by right as the victor. But let me take Patroclus' body back to Achilles."

As Odysseus carried the body of the young hero back to the camp, he dared not imagine the rage that would be unleashed when Achilles realized what had happened.

CHAPTER 5

Achilles versus Hector

Achilles had taken the body of Patroclus into his tent and had not been seen since. They had all seen the column of smoke rising up in the distance, which showed that the funeral fire for Patroclus had been lit. But no one knew what to expect when Achilles finally came out of his tent.

Ajax was worried. "Will he sail home?" He wondered, "He might be tired of war."

Agamemnon was afraid. "He might blame us for Patroclus' death. Will he kill us?"

"Maybe he will just stay in his tent?" Nestor trembled, "He might have gone mad with grief."

Odysseus understood his companions' concerns but shook his head. "I don't think he will do any of those things. We'll just have to wait."

Meanwhile, in Achilles' tent, the hero lay on his bed, looking as though he had not slept in days. There were dark circles around his eyes and his face was gaunt with grief and rage. A warm breeze, as though from the sea, wafted through the tent and he looked up to see his mother, the sea-nymph Thetis, standing there. He leaped to his feet, his jaw-dropping at the sight of what she was carrying. She was holding out new armor, and it was incredible. The chest plate seemed to be made from pure gold. The reflected light from the fire sent dancing stars across the walls and roof of the tent. The helmet was lined with silver and had blood-red rubies set across the forehead. The plume on top seemed to flicker like a flame in the wind. The shield was massive and when it turned towards him he had to cover his eyes, for it shone like the sun.

"My dear son," she said, "I had hoped to spare you the pain of loss by keeping you at home, but destiny, it seems, had other plans for you. You are here now and have much still to do. Do not weep for Patroclus, he died well. Take this armor – I had it made by Hephaistos, god of smiths. Take it, and go forth to victory and glory! Achilles' face broke into the first smile he had worn in what felt like years.

Back in Agamemnon's tent, they were all still waiting for news of Achilles, when the warrior himself finally strode in, clad in his glorious new armor. Agamemnon rose and

The Trojan War

tried to apologize for his actions, but Achilles waved his words aside, looking around the tent at his friends.

"I know why you all look so scared." Growled Achilles. "I swore to have my revenge on you, Agamemnon, for your insult to me. But I have learned that some things are more important than a slave girl. My friend and hundreds of our soldiers are dead because I sat in my tent and did nothing. That blame lies with me alone. I come back to war now to do two things: Kill Hector and burn Troy."

Ever since Hector had killed Patroclus, he had known that the fight with Achilles could not be long delayed. He had lost many brothers and cousins since this terrible war had begun, and he had avenged every single one of them. He remembered the rage and sadness he had felt at seeing their lifeless bodies and knew what Achilles was feeling, knowing that he would not stop until one of them lay dead. As he stood there, men came running back from the direction of the Greek camp. They were scouts he had sent to spy out what was happening. His eyes widened in shock. He had sent twenty men, but only a handful returned. They were crying with terror. "Achilles is coming back to fight!" They shouted as they passed him. "He slew our comrades single-handedly! His rage is like the war god, Ares!" Hector bowed his head, his knuckles tightening on his spear. He could not let any more soldiers die in his place. The time had come to face the great warrior and see who really was the best.

Looking across the plain, he could see something shining, like a comet speeding through the night sky. It must be Achilles. From the top of the walls behind him, he could hear his father and mother begging him to return inside, but he ignored them. He was starting to feel nervous despite himself. The rattle of wheels over stones and earth came to his ears, and within moments, Achilles was leaping down from his chariot, tying the reins to a tree, and striding towards him. He was taller than Hector had imagined. His new armor was certainly impressive, the bronze shone as though it had just been polished, and the shield was broad and strong. But this was not what drew Hector's gaze. Out of Achilles' helmet blazed two pitiless eyes. No man had such eyes. They were full of hatred and grief and rage and bloodlust.

At that moment, Hector's nerve failed him. He turned and ran. Ran as hard as he could. With a cry of rage like a swooping eagle, Achilles sprinted after him. Three times they raced around Troy's high walls. Hector could not escape, but nor could Achilles catch him. As they ran, Achilles could barely believe the speed of Hector. Like a falcon chasing a swallow, like a hound hunting a deer, neither could win and neither could lose. The never-ending war had led to this never-ending chase.

Up on Mount Olympus, the gods had gathered again to watch this great duel. But all were frowning as they saw the two men speeding round and around Troy.

Zeus, the god of lighting and king of the gods, addressed them all. "This is the key moment in this war. Achilles and Hector will fight." He looked around sternly at the other gods, "No one here is to try to change the outcome of this fight. This I decree!" He nodded, and they all felt the clouds and pillars of Olympus shake.

Zeus stared around the room again, and there was a great rumble of thunder overhead as a storm cloud started to form above Olympus. All the other gods glanced nervously at each other. Zeus was enraged. "Athene!" He bellowed. "She had already gone down to Troy before I pronounced my judgment!" Angry as he was, there was nothing even he could do. He was bound by his own decision and could not stop Athene from doing anything. He pounded the arm of his throne and stared down at the two men, still racing around Troy.

As they neared the Scaean gates yet again, Hector thought he saw someone standing ahead of them. With a leap of his heart, he recognized his brother Deiphobus. "Brother!" He called. "You have come at last! We shall face this monster together!" With a mad grin on his face, he skidded to a halt and turned to face Achilles. "It's just you and me now, Hector!" Screamed Achilles, readying his spear. Hector stared at him confused. Did he not see Deiphobus standing a few feet from him? He turned to share the joke with his brother, only to feel terror grab at his heart. Deiphobus' short hair was lengthening before his eyes, his beard fading away. His limbs lengthened till he suddenly towered over Hector, the laughing face of the goddess Athene staring down at him with merciless eyes. The vision was fleeting, and then she was gone, leaving Hector alone before the gates, only a few yards from Achilles, who bayed with laughter.

Realizing that the gods themselves had planned that he and Achilles must fight, he resigned himself to what would come. There was, however, one last thing to say:

"Achilles, I am sorry for taking your friend from you. As was his right, I gave his body back to his people for burial. I respected and honored his memory. If the gods wish me to triumph today, I shall give you the same respect in death. Will you do the same for me? No matter your hatred towards me, can we at least agree on this?"

Achilles raised his helmet. "Look at this face, Hector, and know whom you fight. There are no agreements between lions and men. Tonight, I shall drink to Patroclus' memory, and all shall know what happens to those fools who think they could kill Achilles."

His helmet clanged back into place and Hector knew there was no hope. But he wasn't going to die just standing there. Raising his spear he charged, thrusting forward with all his might. Achilles caught the spear plum in the middle of his shield and the spear shaft shattered in Hector's hand.

"What do you think you can do against me, son of Priam?" Laughed Achilles. "I wear armor made by Hephaistos himself. There is no hope for you!"

Hector glanced at the broken shaft in his hand and tossed it aside. "I will never retreat, Achilles, if you wear armor made by a god, that only shows how much you fear me! Fight me if your dare!"

But even as the Trojan reached for his sword, Achilles ran forwards. Hector desperately raised his own shield as he saw Achilles hurl his spear. The great blade passed straight through Hector's shield, straight through his new armor, and into his heart. Sighing painfully, he slumped to his knees. With his last breath, he whispered, "This place will see your end, too, swift-footed Achilles." And so, Hector died.

Part III

The Fall of Troy

CHAPTER 1

The Grief of King Priam

Achilles stood, breathing heavily, by the corpse of Hector. Without a word or a glance up at the city, he grabbed a rope from his chariot, tied it securely around Hector's ankles, and, urging his horses onwards, dragged Hector's body back to the camp. Looking over his shoulder he could just see the white hair and beard of an old man leaning over the walls of Troy. The winds whipped at Achilles' hair and brought with them a sad cry, a scream of anguish. Priam had watched his son die, and the pain he felt was carried forth on the breeze.

But Priam's pain did not end there. Every day afterward, Achilles pulled the body of Hector behind his chariot round and round Troy and around Patroclus' grave. Such was his own rage and grief at the loss of his dearest friend, Patroclus, that for a while he seemed to have gone mad. But no one in the camp dared question his actions, awful and cruel though they were. With Hector gone, Achilles was, without doubt, the greatest warrior living. None would face his anger or his blade, not even swift Diomedes, mighty Ajax, or wily Odysseus.

Inside the walls of Troy, every man, woman, and child was grieving the loss of their greatest protector. Hector had been like a symbol of hope to them all. Wherever he had gone on the battlefield, the soldiers of Troy had raised their heads and found new strength and bravery seemed to flow through their arms. But he was more than just a great warrior and leader. Few could forget how kind he had been, how helpful. As they sat around the fires in the evening, men of Troy would tell stories not just of his bravery and skill, but of how he had helped them find a lost sheep on Mount Ida, repaired a broken plow, or carried a child home who had got lost in the market and couldn't find his or her mother. Hector had been more than a prince; he had been a good man.

No matter how sad the people of Troy were, their grief was nothing compared to the pain felt by King Priam and Queen Hecuba. Hector's mother had not said a word since the news had reached her. She sat in her room, staring out the window, tears falling constantly down her cheeks. She drank little and ate less. Priam, on the other hand, was the opposite. He cried, of course, but these were tears of rage as well as sadness. He watched Achilles pulling his son's body around Troy every day, and then would run, yelling with fury back to his palace. "Who shall defend us now?" He would cry. "I had fifty sons before the Greeks came to Ilium. Now most of them are gone, but I had hoped that the best of them, dear Hector, would survive." Then his eyes fell on Paris and Deiphobus, the last two of his remaining sons. "Who shall take the crown when I am gone?" He screamed. "Neither of you is worthy. Neither of you is half the man Hector was. Be gone from my sight!"

The two of them turned sadly and left the room, knowing in their hearts both that their father was speaking out of grief and desperation, and also that he was right. Deiphobus was a decent soldier, and Paris was good with a bow and arrow, but neither of them could face any of the great Greek heroes: Diomedes, Ajax, or Odysseus, let alone Achilles.

Down in the city, the wailing cries of women and men alike could still be heard, as well as the sad songs of mourning which would normally be sung at a funeral. But they had no body to bury or burn, so the people of Troy sat around fires, singing sadly, and fearing what new terror would come when the Greeks next attacked their walls. They shared their king's feeling of hopelessness, for none believed that Paris or Deiphobus could take the place of Hector. Meanwhile, Priam continued to switch between rage and grief. Such was his sadness that he could hardly sleep. He would stagger, exhausted, around the walls of Troy, staring out at the distant lights in the dark which showed where the Greeks had made their camp. "I must get my son back." He muttered into his tear-soaked beard. "I must bury him properly." Then a look of resolve came into his eyes. "I must do this, for no one else can."

There came one night without a moon. Into Achilles' tent, there crept a strange old man wearing a hood and cloak. Starting from his seat, the warrior demanded who he was. The old man said nothing but fell to his knees, crawled forwards, and kissed Achilles' hands. Then he pulled back his hood and said, "I am he who has done what no man has ever done before. I have kissed the hands of the man who killed my son."

It took a moment for Achilles to work out what this meant. Then, eyes widening in shock and, surprisingly, terror, he leaped from his seat and backed away. "Priam? How did you even get in here?"

The old man smiled, but it was a smile without happiness, more a sad, knowing look. "No magic or treachery; fear not. I knew this land before you were born to darken it, son of Peleus. And perhaps the gods favored my coming."

Trying to stop his own hands from trembling, Achilles stepped forward, raised Priam from his knees, and sat him in a chair. "You are braver even than any of your soldiers. Why have you come?"

"You know why." The old man's voice trembled. "To ask of you what I should not have to ask. Give me back my son's body! He deserves a decent burial, you know this."

"He killed Patroclus, my best friend!" Snapped Achilles.

Priam stared at him for a moment. "This is war. Men are killed in war; you know this better than anyone. Besides, he thought he was fighting you, and in so doing he sought to protect his people and his home. What do you fight for, Achilles? Glory? Honor? Gold? Your friends and family? You have made a name for yourself as a killer, a soldier, and a leader of men. For these reasons men know your name and give you praise and call you 'hero'. Hector meant just as much to Troy as you do to Greece. What has he done to deserve such treatment at your hands?"

Seeing Achilles' jawline harden, Priam pressed on. "You have heard the story of my father deceiving Herakles, haven't you? Even at the last moment, the greatest hero the world has ever known showed mercy: He let me live. Your father traveled with Herakles for a while, did he not? What would he say, brave Achilles? Would he help you tie my son to your chariot for another ride? Or would he tell you to show mercy?"

Achilles bowed his head, suddenly ashamed. "If I let you take him, we are still enemies. It doesn't change anything."

"Oh, but it does." Replied Priam, slowly. "Before you were hated and feared by all in my city. Now you will just be feared."

"What difference does that make?" Frowned the young Greek.

"Glory is more than having your name remembered, Achilles." Said the old man, rising. "A deed is only great if men think it is great. No one wants to remember an angry boy who dragged a corpse behind a chariot. Don't let that be your legacy."

Achilles rose to face Priam and nodded. "I will prepare your son's body for you. How long do your people need to honor so great a man as Hector?"

Scarcely able to believe it, Priam replied, "Ten days."

Achilles nodded, "Then take twelve. Hector was the best I have ever fought and deserves a hero's funeral to rival that of Herakles'. On my honor, no Greek shall attack Troy in that time. You and your people may mourn Hector in peace."

Priam bowed his thanks. "Be ready to fight on the thirteenth day, son of Peleus."

Agamemnon was not happy that Achilles had promised a twelve-day truce, nor that he had let Priam walk out of the camp without a word but knew better than to argue. No one argued, however, that Achilles had finally done the right thing in returning Hector's body to Priam. So, the army enjoyed a welcome break from the fighting and listened to the sad songs being carried on the wind from Troy. On the third day, they saw a great column of smoke rise from the center of the city and knew that Hector had been sent on his way to the Underworld.

"Stand!" Cried Achilles, marching through the camp. "Stand and remember Hector! He was the best of them, and he died well. We should all hope for such an end, defending our friends and family. His glory shall last forever." And raising a cup of wine to his lips, he toasted his enemy's memory.

CHAPTER 2

The Deaths of Achilles and Paris

For twelve days the Trojans had sung their sad songs, told tales of Hector's bravery, and let their tears flow. Some feared, with their greatest defender gone, that nothing would stop Achilles and Ajax and Odysseus and all the rest from bringing Troy crashing down. But others pointed at the huge walls which stood high and strong around the city. "Even Herakles could not smash those down." They said. "And Achilles is not Herakles."

Meanwhile, in the Greek camp, Agamemnon was urging his council that the time had come for a full assault on the city. "Hector is gone, thanks to Achilles and the Trojans will have no stomach for a fight. They will cower behind their walls, so we must swarm over them and take the city at last. It is time to bring this war to an end!" No one disagreed, and so preparations for the attack began. Swords were sharpened, armor repaired, and long ladders made so that they could climb up over the walls.

On the thirteenth day after Priam had reclaimed his son's body, the Greeks surged towards the city like hundreds of ants. The defenders hurled spears, dropped rocks, and fired arrows down upon them. Even Paris stood there, his great bow bent, firing arrow after arrow at the Greeks. Somehow the ladders were placed at the base of the walls and soldiers started to climb. First among them was Achilles his golden shield held high to protect him from everything the Trojans threw at him. Running round the corner of the nearest tower, Paris watched the great hero climbing.

Knowing that if Achilles could scale the walls, the city would be doomed, Paris fired, but the arrow seemed to just bounce off the hero. Whether the stories about his mother dipping him in the waters of the River Styx, making him invulnerable, were true or whether his armor was simply that strong, Paris didn't know. What he did know was that Achilles was nearly at the top of the ladder! Desperately he fired again, even as a gust of wind flicked his hair into his eyes. The arrow twitched downwards and pierced Achilles' heel. With a scream that echoed off the walls and silenced all who stood near, Achilles fell. With a crash, he hit the ground and moved no more.

Sudden panic seemed to rush through the Greeks as word spread of Achilles' fall. Some threw down their spears and ran; others were seized with rage and threw themselves up the ladders, desperate for revenge, only to be shot down as well. Then mighty Ajax rose, like an oak in a storm, and cried "Hold! Hold! Raise your shields and band together!" Then a warning cry came up from the Scaean gates. They had opened and outpoured a host of Trojans. They were counterattacking! Up on top of the walls, Paris raised a great shout, "Down the ladders, men! Drive these foul Greeks back!"

Odysseus raced to Ajax's side and cried. "We must get the men back or this shall be the end of us all!" Ajax nodded his agreement.

"You carry Achilles, they shall not have him! I'll cover you." He raised his huge shield as Odysseus heaved the great body of Achilles onto his shoulder and, together, they led the men back in slow retreat. "Do not flee, sons of Greece!" Bellowed Ajax, "Do not let them see your backs, or you will feel their spears! We return to the ships, but we leave no man behind!"

They were hard put to it, as the Trojans sallied forth and forced the Greeks back and back. But Paris would not let his men run all the way to the camp. "We have scared them off for now, and I have slain their greatest warrior!" He cried, flushed with triumph. "Tonight, we feast to celebrate our victory, and tomorrow we shall drive them into the sea!" The men about him all cheered and then returned to the city.

The Greeks were somber that evening as they laid Achilles to rest in his tent. They knew that they had no time to bury their comrade properly. The Trojans would be back the next day, Agamemnon was certain, and they had to be ready.

"Of all the things to bring him down," grumbled Diomedes as he, Ajax, and Nestor sat around the fire that evening. "It had to be an arrow of all things?!" That's not the warrior's way. Wherever Achilles' soul is now, I'm sure he's screaming that he should have at least had an honorable death."

Nestor sighed. "This is war, Diomedes, I wouldn't stab a man in the back or while he slept, necessarily, but ultimately, we do what we must to survive until the next awful day. The battle isn't like what the bards sing, it's brutal and bloody. You know this better than anyone."

"I agree with you both," growled Ajax, "but what we must make sure of is that no one else falls to that pesky archer, Paris. Remember how he cowered before Menelaus? That man has no honor. Someone must bring his end before he grows too bold."

At that moment, a man limped out of the shadows.

"A dishonorable, pesky archer, you say?" Came a voice out of the shadows. "Sounds like a job for me!"

"I know that voice." Murmured Diomedes, rising from his seat and staring into the night.

"Oh yes, you do." Snarled Philoctetes as he limped into the firelight. "You'd better since it was you and Odysseus that left me on that damn island, ten years ago!"

All three men's jaws dropped.

"How did you survive? How did you get here?" Stammered Diomedes, taking a step back.

Odysseus stepped into the firelight. "Do you remember that prophecy he claimed to have heard, that Troy would only fall if we had the weapons of Herakles? None of us believed it at the time. I still don't quite believe it now, but now I'm willing to try anything. So, I went back to Lesbos and got him."

"And I nearly shot him." Said Philoctetes with a dirty look at Odysseus. "But I'm a big enough man to accept an apology, and I decided that he wasn't worth one of Herakles' special poisoned arrows in any case. Plus, he promised me my own kingdom when this is all done."

Diomedes glanced at the archer's foot. "Is it healed?"

Philoctetes shook his head. "Not completely, but at least it doesn't stink anymore! Besides, I use my arms to shoot, not my feet."

The next day, Paris himself, resplendent in his finest armor, strode up and down impatiently with his brother, Deiphobus, as the Trojans lined up, ready to sally forth again. His father came to them. "Don't over-reach, Paris." He warned. "You did a great deed yesterday, but don't let it go to your head. The Greeks will not be easy to get rid of."

Paris just smiled at his father. "I'll make you proud, father, never fear!"

As the army marched out, the old king watched his sons go with a sad smile.

Paris was trembling with excitement as they neared the Greek camp. He spread his army out in a great line, then strode forwards into the space between the line and the wall surrounding the Greek camp. "Come out, Greeks!" He cried. "Come out and face us or we shall come in there and chase you out like hounds digging out foxes!" There was no response, so he held up his bow, trying to taunt them. "Are you scared, Greeks? Well, you should be! Here is the bow that killed Achilles! Yes, it was me, Paris, who killed your greatest warrior! He never stood a chance!"

"Oh, shut up, you strutting peacock!" Shouted a coarse voice from the camp. An archer limped into view. "I've got a bow as well, and I'll bet it's got more power than yours! Be off, or you'll hear it sing!"

Paris tried to compose himself. "Is that the only answer you Greeks…"

An arrow whistled through the air and struck him in the shoulder, making him step back at a pace. But the arrow did not pierce his armor. "Come out and face me!" Paris yelled, readying his own weapon as another shaft whizzed past his face! "You missed!" He shouted, suddenly laughing.

"Oh, sorry!" Replied the archer. "How's this?"

This time the arrow struck Paris right on the foot. Crying with pain, he fell to his knees even as his brother ran forward to help him. "What terrible fate is this?" Cried Paris, shaking with agony. His breathing came in gasps, and Deiphobus' eyes widened as he saw his brother's face go first pale and then green. "Poisoned arrows?" He whispered. Without another word, Paris slumped down, dead. Enraged, he turned to the army to call the charge, but another voice echoed out from the camp.

"Hold, prince of Troy! Hear our words!"

Deiphobus recognized the speaker. It was Odysseus.

"Take your brother's body back to his home. We have still to bury Achilles. He allowed you 12 days to honor Hector, please pay us the same courtesy."

Deiphobus looked down at the body of Paris, then silently heaved it onto his shoulders and led the men home.

CHAPTER 3

The Madness of Ajax

>>>> · <<<<

Once the Greeks had laid Achilles' body to rest, toasted his memory, and sung their sad songs, an argument arose over his property. Both Odysseus and Ajax claimed Achilles' armor as their prize, for they alone had rescued Achilles' body from under the hail of arrows at the Scaean gates and brought it safely back to the camp. Agamemnon decided that both men should plead their cases before the whole council of lords. If there was a tie, he would cast the deciding vote.

"I will speak first!" Boomed mighty Ajax. He stood head and shoulders taller than all there and looked slowly around at all present before continuing. "I will speak first, for it is the place of honor. Lord Odysseus is cunning and clever; there's no denying it. But when great Hector, pride of Troy attacked our ships, it was I who stood firm with my shield of bronze and held them off. Indeed, who can forget my great duel with Hector? We fought for a whole day and only the darkness of night ended our epic battle. And who did Hector honor with a gift of a sword? Ajax! I drew blood on him when none of us had managed to do so before, till mighty Achilles brought his end. As for the great act of returning noble Achilles' body, our friend Odysseus carried his great weight gladly, like a donkey!" He paused to laugh. "But it was my shield, my sword, my strength which held back the waves of Trojans as we returned to the camp." Puffing up his massive chest impressively, he barked. "No man here dares test his strength against mine. With Achilles' death, the title of Greece's greatest warrior is passed to me. Therefore, I claim the armor as mine, not just for deeds done, but for honor's sake."

As he rested his great frame back into the chair, Odysseus clapped slowly as he rose to speak. "My good friend, Lord Ajax the mighty, has spoken well." He smiled broadly. "No one can deny what he has done. His bravery and strength are well known. It was a pity that he didn't choose to carry the body and let me deal with the Trojans – I can fight as well as he can, but he'd have borne the weight far more easily. We'd have been back in half the time!"

A few of the lords chuckled at this.

Odysseus continued. "As noble Ajax has said, he drew blood on Hector after a day's long, hard fight. I saw that battle and it was fierce. No wonder it took us ten years to take Troy, with Ajax only cutting someone once a day!" More laughter ensued. Ajax ground his teeth but remained silent.

"But enough of Ajax," said Odysseus calmly as the laughter died away again. "Why am I worthy of Achilles' armor? We have all been here at Ilium for nearly ten, long, painful years. We have all fought. We have all gained prizes and lost friends. My deeds with a sword are well known to all here. But who was it who got Achilles here in the first place? He wouldn't have even been here if it wasn't for me! By whose cunning plans have we so often captured a city or trapped Trojans? Thanks to me and my cleverness, so many more of us stand here alive today. The glory we share, we share because we fought together. But it takes more than a strong arm and a big shield to win a battle, to win a war."

He paused a moment before sitting, and said, "Besides, Achilles and I were about the same size. Can anyone here imagine Ajax squeezing into that armor?"

The tent echoed with roars of laughter as Odysseus, smiling to himself, sat down. Agamemnon, laughing so hard that tears rolled down his cheeks, asked all to be quiet again, but it took a while. "My lords, it is time to vote. All those in favour of giving the armor to Ajax?" Ajax glanced around the circle; hands were going up. He couldn't count quickly enough before Agamemnon continued, "And all those in favour of Odysseus?" The same number of hands seemed to rise into the air and Agamemnon sighed. "A draw." He paused; eyes closed in thought. "I choose Odysseus." All rose to clap Odysseus on the back and applaud him. Meanwhile, Ajax, forgotten, sat motionless in his chair, his knuckles white as he gripped his knees, his eyes wide and staring. Unable to even look at Odysseus' sneering, triumphant face, he stomped out of the tent.

That night, Ajax lay tossing and turning in his bed, growling, and pummelling his pillow. He kept muttering random phrases: "Dishonoured me!" "Not a fair contest." "Should have fought for it. Should have fought for it." "I'll show them." While in his mind he could not rid himself of the sight and sound of all those lords laughing. They pointed at him, hooting with glee, some rolling on their backs holding their sides as he tried in vain to pull the armor of Achilles over his head. Then Odysseus' face loomed out in front of him, and he snatched wildly at it, but always Odysseus seemed just a little out of reach, laughing derisively. "I'll show you all!" Roared Ajax, leaping out of bed. Grabbing his sword, he stumbled from his tent. The night seemed hazy before him, as though fog from the sea had floated in. Blundering through the camp, he kept running into trees or tripping over tent ropes.

Finally, he found what he was looking for: Agamemnon's tent. Forcing his way inside, he found them all there: Odysseus and Agamemnon and Diomedes and Menelaus and all the rest. They just stared glumly at him, not moving. "You thought you could dishonor me!" Bellowed Ajax, raising his sword. "Now feel my wrath, you pigs!" And he killed them all. Some ran around, bleating and screaming but none raised a sword in defense. Ajax laughed as he slew. He was like a god of war; none could defeat him. Breathing hard, he pulled his sword from the last body and backed away. Then a voice made him whip around.

"Ajax!" The stunned voice of Odysseus echoed through the night. "What have you done?"

Ajax stared at him in confusion. He had just killed him, hadn't he? He turned around. The tent had disappeared, but the blood that soaked the ground and was splashed all over Ajax's arms and sword remained. More people were appearing out of the darkness, carrying torches and by their light, Ajax saw the massacre before him. Dozens of sheep lay dead on the ground before him. He had stumbled, not into the tent of Agamemnon, but into the pens where the sheep were kept at night.

"Ajax…" Odysseus said, slowly. "Are you ok?"

Trembling with emotion, Ajax began to weep. "No… I, I killed you." He took a step away. "I killed you, Odysseus."

Odysseus shook his head, unsmilingly. "No, you didn't my friend. You're a good man, you would never…"

"I killed you!" Bellowed Ajax hysterically. "And you!" He pointed at Agamemnon. "And you, Menelaus. I killed all of you!"

"It was a dream, Ajax." Said Odysseus soothingly. "A terrible nightmare. You didn't mean to do it. We're your friends. We're here for you. Come." He offered his hand. "Come sit by the fire and we'll talk."

"No!" Ajax backed away further, tripping over a dead sheep. "I'll just hurt you all again." Tears were flooding down his cheeks. "What have I done?!"

"Nothing!" Cried Agamemnon, striding forward to stand by Odysseus. "You have done nothing wrong, noble Ajax. This war has had a terrible impact on you and on us all. But we can help you get through this, my friend. Trust us, as we trust you."

But Ajax shook his great head. "No. I can't. Not after this. I'm a danger to you all. I'm sorry."

And before anyone could stop him, Ajax had turned his sword point toward his chest and fallen forwards, driving the blade straight through his heart.

All stood in silence around the body of the fallen warrior. "He didn't deserve this end." Shuddered Odysseus, tears falling down his cheeks. "We must all look to our friends, our brothers in arms, lest more take their own lives in hopelessness and despair." In the half-light of the stars and moon, he could just see the city of Troy, dark against the night sky. He shook his fist at it, saying, "I wish we had never come here. But here we are, and I'll be damned if we lose another life so needlessly. Somehow, Troy must fall."

CHAPTER 4

The Wooden Horse

It was with heavy hearts that the Greeks laid Ajax the mighty to rest. They had lost so many during the last ten years, but this death felt different. Odysseus still shuddered when he remembered the hopelessness, the sadness, and the self-hatred in Ajax's voice. Looking around the fire that evening at his fellow lords, he wondered how many of them were feeling as lonely and dejected as Ajax must have felt. There had to be a way into Troy. Herakles had done it, so surely so could they? Both sides had suffered greatly in battle, the men had no energy or enthusiasm for yet another all-out assault on the walls.

"You've got that look on your face." Diomedes' voice cut through his thoughts. "Like just before you suggested we make that night raid. It's the "this is going to sound crazy but hear me out" look. Come on then – spit it out."

Odysseus looked around the circle of expectant faces and sighed. He had had so many good ideas before, that they all expected him to pull something incredible out of his helmet. Taking a deep breath, he explained his idea.

The Fall of Troy

"We can't take Troy with a direct assault, so we've got to trick them into letting us in themselves. We build a huge statue out of wood, hide some men inside it, and the rest of the army pretend to leave. They sail away and hide the fleet behind an island, Tenedos maybe. We will need someone to remain behind, pretending to have been abandoned. They will tell the Trojans that the statue is an offering to Poseidon, god of the sea, for a safe voyage home. The Trojans respect the gods–they will want to take the statue into their city to the temple of Poseidon. Once night has fallen, the men inside the statue sneak out, open the gates, and let the army in, who will have returned under cover of darkness."

There was a stunned silence Agamemnon looked at his brother, Diomedes raised his eyes at Nestor, and Nestor looked thoughtfully at Odysseus.

It was Agamemnon who broke the silence.

"It is a crazy idea. So crazy that it just might work. We'll start building the statue tomorrow. What shape should it be?"

Odysseus thought for a moment. "A horse. They're sacred to Poseidon and they're a symbol of Priam's family."

Agamemnon smiled. "If this works, Odysseus, your name will be remembered forever."

Three days later, a group of scouts came from Troy to check on the Greek camp, as they had many times before. But this time was different. Where the Greek camp had stood was now empty, save for bits of rubbish and the remains of fires. The great gouge marks in the sand where the ships had stood for so long were still there, but there was no sign of the men who had plagued their land for so long. Silently, they gave the gods thanks, and then cast their eyes over the gigantic form which cast a shadow over them. The great wooden horse had been fashioned out of old pieces of ship timbres, tent poles, and driftwood, as well as freshly felled trees. It was a marvel to behold. One of them rode back to the city to tell the king the wonderful news. Within hours, Priam rode down to the shore to see what he had barely been able to believe. "It's a miracle." He whispered, staring around the deserted beach, and up at the massive statue.

At that moment, there was a commotion close at hand, some of Priam's guards came forward, dragging a man with them. As they threw him down, they saw that he only had one eye. "Let me go, please!" He shouted then, seeing Priam, he threw himself on the floor and begged. "Great king, please! Let me go!"

Priam frowned. "Who are you, Greek? Why are you still in Ilium, when all your comrades have left?"

The man replied, trembling, "Sinon, son of Aesimus. I am here because I am already a cursed man." He gestured to his missing eye. "Some god sent a sickness that caused my eye to go bad. The healers had to remove it, but they warned that the sickness could return. Odysseus, that sly, thieving, lying dog, he persuaded King Agamemnon that I was cursed, that my sickness would spread to the other ships. So, they left me behind."

Priam stared at the man, a pang of sympathy rising in his chest. "What of this horse?" He gestured to the great wooden statue. "Why is it here?"

"An offering, great king," explained Sinon, "to Poseidon, so that he would grant them a safe journey home."

A raucous laugh echoed along the shore, and all turned to see whose it was. Laocoon, a priest of Apollo, had pushed his way to the front of the crowd accompanying Priam. "You don't really believe him, my king? No Greek can be trusted!" He cried, pointing at Sinon. "Troy will never be safe so long as a single Greek remains alive on our shores. I fear them with every bone in my body – even when they come bearing such a gift for the gods as this. Burn the horse, my lord, and burn this liar with it!"

He grabbed a spear from one of the guards and hurled it at the horse. It struck the great wooden belly with a deep thud that echoed inside it.

Even as the noise died away, a new sound came to their ears. A horrible, sucking, splashing rush made the hairs on their heads stand on end. Turning towards the seashore, a dozen paces away, they watched in horror as a great sea serpent rose out of the waves and slithered up the beach towards Laocoon. The man tried to run, but the snake was too swift. Wrapping its coils around him, it pulled him to the ground and then dragged him back into the waves, even as he screamed and fought with all his might. Priam's horse neighed with terror and would have bolted if he hadn't managed to calm it.

All the men were backing away from the sea and the statue, terror etched on every face. "It's true then!" Cried one of the men. "Poseidon has blessed the Greeks with a safe journey home and will kill any man who harms the statue!"

Priam's frown deepened. He looked up at the horse for a moment, then down at Sinon.

"Release him." He ordered. "I never want to see you again, Greek. Your people have done enough damage to my land."

"What of the horse, lord king?" Asked one of the guards.

"It is a gift for the great god Poseidon, to damage it would bring his wrath down on us as well. Bring it into the city and take it straight to the temple of Poseidon. I will find the priests and arrange our own sacrifices to the god of the sea. We must make sure that Laocoon's insult to the god has been repaid fully."

It took most of the day to drag

the great, wooden statue inside the city. Hundreds of Trojans flocked out of the city to watch and help. Many cried with happiness at the sight of it. They sang and danced and feasted for the whole day and well into the night. As midnight came, all of Troy slept deeply. Not a soul moved. Then came a creak of wood, like a door opening. A hole appeared in the belly of the wooden horse and a rope was lowered. Silently, Odysseus climbed down and glanced around. The streets were empty, and the way was clear. Beckoning to the others to follow him, he ran stealthily towards the main gates. A few sleepy guards sat round a fire. They all died silently with hands clamped over their mouths to stop them from crying out. Heaving the gates open, Odysseus took a burning torch and waved it above his head. Within moments he could hear the low rumbling of thousands of feet approaching. He saw the moonlight glinting off spears and helmets.

The first to enter was Agamemnon, closely followed by Menelaus and Diomedes. The four of them stood together for a moment, framed in the open gates, savoring this moment of triumph.

"Would you care to give the order, mighty king?" Asked Odysseus, smiling at Agamemnon. The two of them had not always seen eye to eye, but they had been through a great deal together.

Agamemnon returned the grin and raised his voice so that all could hear him, "Sons of Greece, your hour has come! Burn it all! Take what you can!"

CHAPTER 5

Aeneas' Flight from Troy

>>>> · <<<<

"Wake up, son of Anchises!" Aeneas' heart was in his mouth as he sat up in bed. Immediately he could tell that something was wrong. The smell of smoke was heavy in the air, blowing through the open window. He stared around to see who had spoken, and nearly fainted at what he saw. In the doorway to his room stood Hector, son of Priam. Aeneas blinked and shook his head, but still, could he see Hector, indistinct, blurred, and yet shining, like the moon seen through heavy fog. "What is this, a dream?" Asked Aeneas of the ghost before him.

Hector shook his head, sadly. "Alas not, my friend. I am here to warn you: Troy has fallen. The horse which my father allowed into the city was a trick – men were concealed inside, and they opened the gates. Greeks are in the city."

At these words, Aeneas leaped out of bed, his quick ears suddenly alert to the sounds of screaming and the clang of weapons outside. He hurriedly reached for his armor, but Hector raised his hand. "It is too late, Aeneas. Troy has fallen. You must escape. Take your son, your family, and as many of our people as you can and flee. There will be a new home for our people beyond Ilium, but you must go now!" With these last, echoing words, Hector faded into nothingness.

Fastening his armor, Aeneas roused his wife. "Creusa! Hurry! Get Ascanius, I will wake my father. The Greeks have entered the city and we must flee. There is no time to waste!"

Her eyes were wide with terror, but she did as he instructed. Aeneas ran from the room, calling for his father. The old man was hard to awaken, but he reacted quickly when he saw his son's fearful expression and smelled the smoke in the air.

Many of the houses on their street were already burning. Men ran this way and that, women cried, and children screamed. Anchises had Ascanius by either hand. Aeneas called to some other Trojans who running towards them. "Hold! We must flee! The Greeks are in the city. Take those women and lead them to the Temple of Apollo, it's the furthest from the main gates."

But then a scream much closer at hand made him spin around. Several Greeks had charged around a building and, seeing the group of them standing there, attacked. One was an archer who shot several arrows at them. Raising his shield, Aeneas bellowed as he ran forwards, slicing and stabbing with his sword. They were good fighters, but none were a match for him. Once they were all dead, Aeneas turned to see where his family was. With a sudden shock, he realized that his wife was not there. "Where is Creusa?" He cried. Anchises shook his head – he had no idea.

Rage and fear such as Aeneas had never known before surged through him. "Take Ascanius and head to the temple." He told his father. "Gather as many of our people as you can."

His father shouted something, but Aeneas was already running, his eyes burning, his hands shaking. He heard the screams and more sounds of swords clashing up ahead. Following the noise, he found several Greeks and Trojans fighting. Roaring like a wounded lion, he hurled himself into the midst of the battle. His sword shone like red lightning in the light of the fires. No one seemed able to stand against him. Collecting more and more men as he went, Aeneas led a desperate, running fight through Troy. Part of his mind was wondering where Sinon was, that treacherous, lying coward who had tricked Priam into letting the wooden horse inside. More Greeks fell to his blade, but still, that thunderous pounding of his heart would not stop.

As he came near the palace, Aeneas saw, in the distance, a small group of Trojans desperately fighting to defend the temple of Zeus. An old man knelt on the steps of the temple, sword in hand, praying. Behind him stepped a great Greek warrior, holding a spear. Even from this distance, Aeneas could recognize that lion-topped helmet. It was Agamemnon, king of Mycenae, and the old man praying was King Priam. With his heart in his mouth he ran forward but knew he would be too late.

The Fall of Troy

Priam turned from his prayer and saw Agamemnon approaching. With a deep sigh, he hefted the sword in his old, white hands and faced his enemy. "You have won, Agamemnon." He wheezed as the smoke wreathed about them. "Why slaughter my people? Spare them, please."

Agamemnon smiled cruelly. "We have been here for ten years, Priam. My men will accept nothing less than total victory. That means Troy is in ruins." He raised the spear. "That means your blood on my blade."

Priam gripped his sword in both hands, his eyes blazing. "I fought alongside Perseus and Cadmus, the greatest monster slayers of their time. You are nothing more than another foul creature, ready to be put down."

Agamemnon laughed. "Try me." And with that, he lunged at Priam, who stepped aside and swung with his sword. But his old arms were tired and weak, and the sword merely glanced off Agamemnon's armor. The next spear thrust caught Priam in the shoulder knocking him to the floor. Blood trickled down the temple steps as Agamemnon stood over the old king and stabbed down one more time. Aeneas cried aloud as he saw Priam's old body go limp. But he was too far away, and more Greeks were flooding up the temple's steps. There were too many of them, even for him. Fresh tears in his eyes, he turned and led his men away, still searching for his wife.

Passing by a burning house, he skidded to a halt as he heard someone call his name. Squinting through the ash and dust which hung in the air, his heart finally stopped pounding. His mouth went dry, and he almost dropped his sword in shock. Creusa, his wife, was standing in the doorframe of a house. He ran towards her, but his hands passed through hers as though they were made of smoke. "Not another ghost!" he whispered. Creusa's spirit nodded.

"I am dead, my dear Aeneas. Troy is burning." She looked around sadly at the house and the city beyond it. "You have saved many lives already, but you cannot save them all. My death was not your fault. No matter how many Greeks you kill, I cannot come back, and you will not feel any better."

Aeneas bowed his head; he knew she was right.

"But there is more that you can do, my dear husband! Our son needs his father. More than that: He needs a new home. Our people need a new home. You must go to Italy, to the place where a great river passes seven hills. Then you will find peace. Go Aeneas! Go now!"

And with these final words, she faded away, as the ghost of Hector had done.

The Trojans who stood with Aeneas gaped at him as he turned around. "Lord Aeneas…" Said one of them, trembling. "What was that?"

Aeneas smiled at the man. "That, my friend, was destiny revealing itself to us." He called to the other warriors standing nearby. "Sons of Troy! You have fought bravely. For ten years you have fought bravely. But we could not stop destiny. Troy was meant to fall, but out of the ashes, it shall rise again. We must leave. We will sail away and find ourselves a new home. Come with me now. Kill any Greek who stands in our way, save any fellow Trojan that you can, but do not stop. Troy is dead, but we Trojans can still live!"

So began the final escape. Aeneas and his men charged through Troy like a river. Nothing could stop them, though many Greeks died trying. On arriving at the temple of Apollo, they found many others: men, women, and children, already waiting there. Organizing the soldiers into a rear guard and a forward line, with those who could not fight safely in the middle, Aeneas led them on away from the temple. Whether because some god had helped them, or because the Greeks had not yet got to this part of the city, but they found no more attackers. The way to the gates was clear. As they fled out of the city and towards Troy's harbor, Aeneas turned and looked back. All of Troy was burning now, a huge, black pillar of smoke blotting out the stars and even the moon. Tears were pouring down his face at the sight of his home in ruins. But the voices of Hector and Creusa came back to him.

"There will be a new home for our people beyond Ilium."

"Go to Italy, to the place where a great river passes seven hills."

Aeneas raised his sword to the sky. "I will go to Italy!" He cried aloud. "With the gods and my people as witnesses, I swear that I will find us a new home!"

Part IV

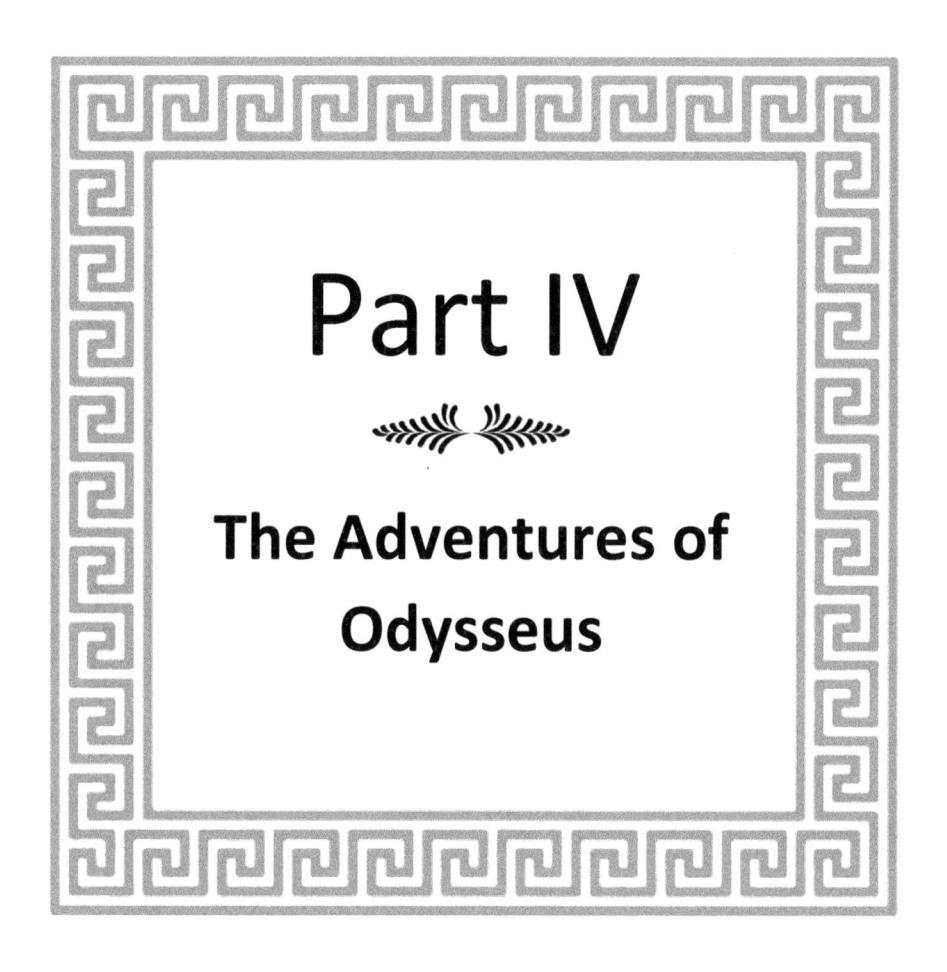

The Adventures of Odysseus

The Adventures of Odysseus

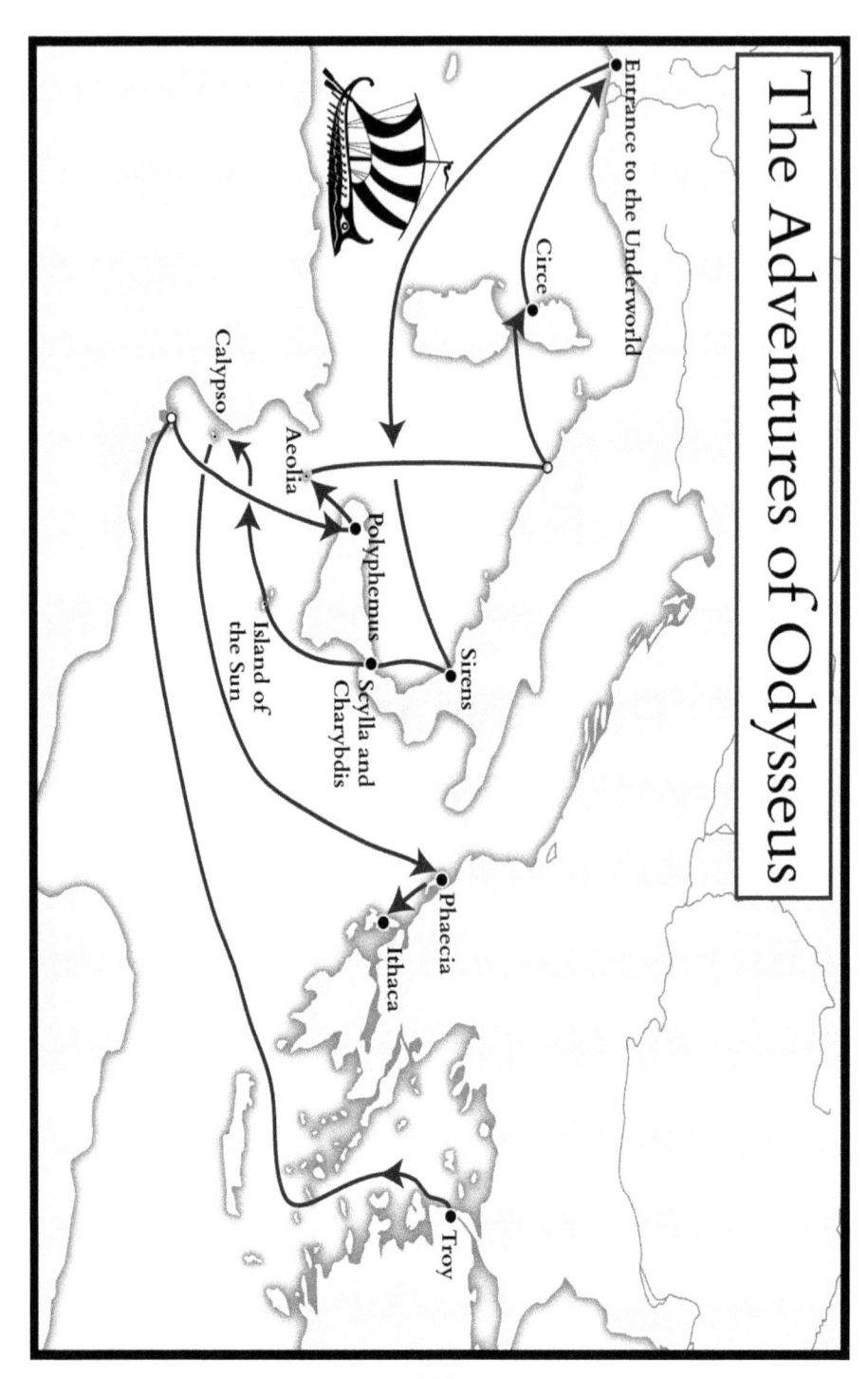

CHAPTER 1

Polyphemus

>>>> · <<<<

Odysseus stood at the front of his flagship, ahead of the other eleven ships he had brought with him to Troy ten years before. Next to him stood Eurylochus, his brother-in-law and second-in-command, who asked. "Happy to be finally sailing home, my lord?"

Odysseus grinned. "Ask me again when we reach Ithaca. This war should have taken ten weeks, not ten years. I don't want to tempt fate!"

Eurylochus laughed "Oh come on. You conquered Troy! I think you'll be able to lead us back home without much trouble!"

With that, Eurylochus gave the order to raise the sail and signaled to the rest of the ships to follow. They were off! Odysseus raised his eyes to the sky and said a quiet prayer to Poseidon, god of the sea:

"Oh mighty Poseidon, lord of the wine-dark sea,

I have always honored you with sacrifices,

The Adventures of Odysseus

And it was by your symbol of the horse that we took Troy.

Your power over the sea knows no limits. Please hear my prayer:

Let me bring my men safely home and I shall place half my gold from Troy in your temples on Ithaca."

High up on Mount Olympus, Poseidon and Athena, goddess of wisdom, heard Odysseus' prayer and looked down on the tiny speck which was his ship. They glanced sadly at each other, for both knew that Odysseus was fated not to return home for a long time. "Destiny is a cruel thing." Said Athena, her brow furrowed.

"It is," agreed Poseidon. "But this voyage will raise Odysseus' name higher than any other hero. He shall be remembered forever."

Nearly a week after leaving the shores of Ilium, fog rolled in from the west like a great wall. Odysseus called to his other ships, ordering them to lower their sails and use their oars, keeping them together as best as possible so as not to lose each other in the fog. The night flowed over them, and still, the fog held on, blocking out the stars and even the moon. As dawn brought a cold, damp light to their world again, the fog remained but somehow, three of the ships had disappeared out of sight and calling distance. Odysseus' heart was heavy. He had a duty to bring these men home safely, and this was not a good start. Then Eurylochus, who was on watch at the prow of the ship, called "Land! I can see land ahead!"

Odysseus rushed forwards and squinted through the cold, wet whiteness of the fog. A dark shape was looming out of the fog ahead, and he could hear waves lapping against the murky shore. Clapping Eurylochus on the shoulder and smiling, he sent word back to the other ships that they should all moor on the shore ahead, and there they would wait for the fog to lift before heading onwards.

"We can get fresh supplies, too." He continued. "Water, and whatever berries, nuts, or animals we can find." Turning to the men he called. "Bring five sacks of wine – if we find anyone, we can trade it for what we need."

As they walked, they found no walls or fences to keep the herds in place, nor were there any crops. Odysseus was puzzled. "What kind of wild men live here?" He wondered aloud. Then one of his men, a cheerful man called Polites, pointed ahead to where a hill stood. In the steep, rocky slope there was a large, dark hole gaping wide like a huge mouth, beside which stood a massive stone. "A cave, my lord! And there is smoke coming out of it!"

Odysseus nodded. "That must be where they live, whomever they are."

Carefully, they entered the great cave. As their eyes got used to the light, they saw an empty sheep pen; several dozen sheep skins laid out on the floor, like a huge bed; and ten or twelve huge clay pots. It took two men together to lift the lid of one of these, to discover that they contained creamy, white cheese.

"Don't take any!" Cried, Odysseus. "We are already impolite by entering their home. We should wait for them to return before eating anything.

They did not have long to wait. The bleating of sheep announced the arrival of the cave's inhabitants. Turning to the doorway to greet their hosts, Odysseus' jaw dropped as he saw what came it. The sheep were normal-sized, but the shepherd was monstrous. Easily three times the height of a normal man he towered over them. He entered the cave backward, dragging a whole tree with him. Once inside, he rolled the great stone in front of the doorway, sealing the entrance. A little light came in over the top of the boulder, and the smoke from the fire was able to escape too, but there was no way they could get out. Odysseus' men clustered together behind him as the monster turned. One more surprise lay in store: His face was ugly, rough, and dirty, but he had only one eye, right in the middle of his forehead.

"It's a cyclops!" Whispered Polites, his voice trembling. "We're done for!"

The cyclops' eye widened with rage and surprise as he caught sight of the intruders in his cave.

"Who are you?" He boomed with a voice like thunder.

Odysseus thought quickly, there was only one chance of escape. "My name is Nobody. What's yours, noble cyclops?"

The cyclops smiled wickedly. "I am Polyphemus, son of the sea god Poseidon, and you look tasty…" Suddenly he reached out and grabbed one of Odysseus' men. The man screamed and kicked, but the cyclops was too strong. Cramming the man into his mouth, Polyphemus swallowed him whole. The others drew their swords and would have attacked if Odysseus had not stopped them.

He turned back to Polyphemus, who was picking at his uneven teeth with one massive, muddy finger. "Great Polyphemus, may I offer you a gift?" The cyclops stopped picking and stared down at the hero with his single, dark eyeball. "What gift?"

Odysseus brought him the sacks of wine. He unfastened the stopper on one, and handed it to Polyphemus who sniffed it curiously, then drank the whole bagful in two great gulps.

"Argh," he grunted. "That's good. More!"

Smiling broadly, Odysseus handed the cyclops another bag of wine, and then another. As he finished the third wine sack, the great eyelid began to droop.

"Another…" he mumbled as he sat down on his bed of sheepskins. Odysseus handed him the fourth and final sack.

The monster drank it and then lay back with a grunting sigh. Within moments, the cave was echoing with his thunderous snores.

Polites and Amphialos rushed forward, swords in hand, but Odysseus pushed them back.

"But lord," snarled Amphialos, "you've done it! Now the monster is asleep we can kill him easily and revenge our comrade."

Odysseus raised his eyebrows, "Clever plan. And once he's dead you shall just put your shoulder to the great stone and we'll all walk out of here, I suppose."

Amphialos' mouth opened and closed a couple of times. "How can we move the stone, then?"

"We can't." Answered Odysseus simply. "But he can." He pointed at the cyclops. In hushed tones, he gathered his men together and explained his plan.

Together they hacked off a branch from the tree Polyphemus had brought inside. Then they sharpened one end until it was pointed like a spear. As the moon rose in the night sky outside, it shone down upon the sleeping cyclops. Odysseus and his men lifted the great weapon, and charged at the cyclops, aiming for his single eye.

There was a horrible scream as the cyclops awoke. They all backed against the cave walls, dodging out of the way of the great hands as the monster crawled around the cave, roaring with pain and rage. Outside they heard another cyclops stomp over and shout. "What is wrong, Polyphemus?"

Polyphemus crawled around and bellowed. "Nobody has blinded me, brother!"

There was a pause, and then the other cyclops answered, "Brother, you are sick! You're not making any sense at all! Stay in there until you are well."

Odysseus listened to the heavy footsteps leaving and breathed a sigh of relief. So far, his plan was working.

The next morning, the sheep were milling around the doorway, bleating to go out. Polyphemus blindly felt his way over and pushed the stone out of the way. But then he sat at the cave's mouth, waving his hands slowly over the sheep to make sure no man snuck out. "I will find you. I will find you!" growled the cyclops as he felt the soft woolen backs of the sheep slide under his great dirty hands. Little did he know, however, that Odysseus and his men had taken sheepskins from the bed and covered themselves with them. Dressed as sheep, they crawled out, making soft bleating noises. Once they were far enough away, Odysseus stood up and shouted back at the cyclops. "Ha, foolish monster! My name is Odysseus, not Nobody. You can never catch us now!" Roaring with laughter, he and his men herded the sheep down the slope. Behind them, they could hear the cyclops bellowing with rage. "Father!" he cried, "Great god Poseidon, curses Odysseus to the depths of the sea!"

Odysseus and his return to the ship with the sheep and set sail, still laughing.

I hope you've enjoyed the book.
Please kindly leave a review:

CHAPTER 2

The Bag of Winds

≫≫≫ · ≪≪≪

As they sailed away from the island of the cyclops Polyphemus, Odysseus and his men held a moment of silence in honor of the crewman, Inacus, who had been eaten by the monster. They had lost many friends over the years at Troy, but losing another comrade to such a creature was somehow worse. Lycaon the flute player played a sad tune that was taken away by the wind. Once he was finished, the first to speak was Eurylochus. "Where to now then, Odysseus? I'm guessing that cyclops didn't tell you which way we need to go?"

Odysseus scowled at Eurylochus, but it was a fair question. "We go west, Ithaca should lie in that direction still. With that, Polites took the helm and steered the ship as ordered.

A few days later, they came to another island. Once all the ships were safely moored, Odysseus led a band of men, up away from the shore. After maybe half an hour of walking uphill, the path flattened out, and they could see a large, well-built house ahead of them. Before they could even knock, however, the great, oaken doors swung open and a tall man with hair and beard as wispy-white as clouds came out. He raised his hands and smiled at them. "Welcome!" He cried. "Welcome to Aeolia! I am Aeolus."

Odysseus looked a little confused. "I'm sorry? I've never heard of Aeolia. We must be a little off course."

Aeolus' smile broadened. "Not to worry, mighty Odysseus. Come inside. I would gladly hear your tales, and I'm sure you and your men wouldn't say no to a cup of wine."

"How do you know my name?" Asked Odysseus, slightly worried.

Aeolus winked. "Let's just say that the winds brought it to me."

Once inside, they were all served deep cups of excellent wine, and Aeolus asked Odysseus a thousand questions about Troy, of which he seemed to know a great deal already.

"I do love hearing things from people who were actually there!" He said enthusiastically. "I never leave my island, so it's wonderful to experience things at least second-hand."

Night had fallen by the time Aeolus stopped questioning Odysseus, and the hero was exhausted. Standing, he staggered slightly due to the amount of wine he had drunk. Half of his men were asleep in their chairs.

"Now!" Cried Aeolus. "Now that you have told me such wonderful tales, it is time for me to give you a gift, Odysseus! Come with me."

He led him to a balcony that overlooked the wide, dark sea. Taking a large, empty wine sack from one of his servants, Aeolus held his arm aloft.

"What are you doing?" Asked Odysseus, completely confused.

Aeolus winked at him again. "I told you the winds brought me your name. I am more than just a man with good wine, Odysseus. I am Aeolus, the god of the winds, and I wish to speed you on your way." There was a sudden rushing noise, and Odysseus was almost blown over as the wind gushed toward them. Shielding his eyes with his hand, Odysseus watched open-mouthed as Aeolus held the wine sack above his head and then crammed the stopper shut. "I have captured all the winds except for the west wind." He explained. "You are a long way off course, as you guessed, but in nine days, the west wind will blow you straight to Ithaca. Don't open it again until you are safely ashore at home!"

Odysseus' eyes widened and he could not thank Aeolus enough, but the god waved his thanks away and then helped him wake his slumbering men.

Dashing down to the ships, Odysseus called excitedly that they should cast off immediately.

Eurylochus frowned. "What's in that bag?" He eyes the heavy wine sack curiously.

Odysseus smiled. "The fog is already blowing away. And I will tell you what's in the sack once we get home, not before! It's a wonderful surprise, and you wouldn't believe me even if I told you!" He was grinning from ear to ear as they all climbed on board and raised the sails.

Eurylochus scowled but did as he was told. A strong wind was making the sails billow and snap as the ships turned. Then they surged forward into the night, as the stars glinted overhead, and the moon smiled down on them.

Eight days later, however, Eurylochus' patience was wearing thin. Odysseus had promised them all that they would soon be home, but they had been sailing west for so long. "We can't have been that far off course!" He said to himself. "And what is in that sack? Why won't he tell even just me?! I'm the closest thing he has to an actual brother. After all, we've been through, he could at least tell me, even if he wants to keep it a secret from the men." But whenever he asked Odysseus, the hero just smiled and said, "Wait and see."

That night, Eurylochus lay in his bunk, tossing and turning. He could not seem to get comfortable. His fingers twitched and every noise on the ship seemed louder than normal. But there was something else that kept him awake. It was as though there was a small voice in his head, or perhaps it came from the waves outside, which kept saying to him, "Look in the bag. Open it. See what's inside!" Finally, he could not resist the temptation any longer. He sneaked over to where Odysseus slept, gently raised the sack out of the hero's sleepy arms, and pried the stopper out. The world seemed to turn itself upside down. Winds blasted the ship from every side. The sail ripped in two, half the men were hurled overboard and there was a great crashing of wooden timbers. All the crew were awake now, and they watched in horror as the rest of the fleet were smashed into each other, several of the ships sinking before their very eyes. Then their craft was spun around like a feather and hurled away far across the sea. In what direction, no one knew.

When the ship finally came to rest, Odysseus was the first to find his balance. They had been spinning round and around for so long, that none of them knew which way was which.

"Who opened the bag?" Odysseus shouted, staring around at his men. Those that were able to stand looked at him, dumbfounded. "Who opened the bag?!" He roared, slamming his fist into the mast.

Eurylochus stepped forwards. "A better question, Odysseus, is why you didn't tell us about the bag? Why didn't you explain to us why it should not be opened?!"

Odysseus stared at him. "This isn't my fault! When I make a decision, I expect you all to accept it. One more day and we would have been safe at home. One of you betrayed the rest of us. I want to know who did this." He glared around at the rest of the crew.

Eurylochus ground his teeth. In his heart, he knew that he was to blame, but he was too scared to admit it. So instead, he said, "We've just lost most of our fleet, we've no idea where we are, and you are just pointing fingers and blaming others. Why don't we focus instead on staying alive and finding our way home?"

Odysseus couldn't argue with this, but he was still angry. But more than being angry, he was afraid. He could still hear, as though the wind and waves were carrying the words to him, the bellowing rage of Polyphemus the cyclops: "Great god Poseidon, curse Odysseus to the depths of the sea!"

"Have I doomed my friends?" He wondered. "Was this a betrayal by one of my men, or was it the will of the gods?" He shook himself slightly and set to helping his men as they repaired the ship.

CHAPTER 3

Circe

>>>> · <<<<

For several days, they sailed onward, grateful for the sheep and water they had gained from Polyphemus' island. Finally, they sighted another island and steered towards it. As they neared the shore, Eurylochus took Odysseus aside. "I'm leading the party ashore this time, Odysseus."

Eyes narrowing with fury, Odysseus asked "Why? I'm in charge here, I lead the men."

"Your last two trips have ended in disaster and death." Replied Eurylochus angrily. "I'll see if I can break our bad luck and get us some answers."

Odysseus scowled for a moment but finally growled, "Fine. You try your best, and if I have to come and save you, I won't hear another word from you."

The night was nearly upon them as they moored the ship in a small, rocky bay, so it wasn't until the next morning when Eurylochus led Polites, Alkimos, and a half dozen others off into the hills which surrounded them. All day

Odysseus waited. He tried to keep himself busy, doing odd jobs around the ship, refilling all the waterskins at a small stream halfway up the slope, but his eyes kept searching the hills. He was so worried about Eurylochus and the rest that as evening began to draw in, he made ready to go looking for them.

He was just fastening his sword belt when a shout from the slope above made his heart leap. Eurylochus was running down the slope, his eyes wide and fearful. "Odysseus!" He called. The hero leaped off the ship and ran to meet him.

"Eurylochus! Where are the others?"

Eurylochus fell to his knees before Odysseus and began to weep. "Odysseus – we must leave this place. This island is the home of a witch. We approached her house and heard her singing. She invited us in but sensing something was wrong I hid and did not enter. Watching through the window, I saw her pour each of our comrades a cup of some potion. As each drank they began to snort with laughter, then each turned into a pig before my eyes!" He howled with despair and buried his face in his hands.

Odysseus stared at him for a second, barely able to believe his wild story. But he had known Eurylochus for many years and knew that he wasn't a liar or one to imagine things.

"Go back to the ship, if I don't return by this time tomorrow, sail away." And with that, he headed off into the hills, retracing his men's steps.

As he climbed higher into the woods, he felt the hairs on the back of his neck standing up on end. Someone or something was watching him. He drew his sword and stared around into the darkness. Then, from behind a tree, there came a silvery laugh. Out strode a young man who seemed to shine a pale gold, like the sun on the sand. Odysseus stepped back a pace. "Who are you?"

The young man smiled. "I am Hermes, the messenger of the gods." It was then that Odysseus noticed the small wings on Hermes' sandals, which were said to grant him the power to fly faster than the swiftest bird on the strongest wind. He bowed his head.

"What brings the messenger of the gods to me?" His heart leaped. "Does mighty Zeus send me a word? Have you come to guide me home?"

Hermes grinned sadly. "Alas, no, wily Odysseus. I just happened to be passing by and caught wind of your little problem with the witch Circe. I have a gift for you and some advice."

Trying to conceal his disappointment, Odysseus bowed again. "Thank you. Please, speak on."

Hermes held out a small plant with black roots and white leaves. "Eat this, it will protect you from Circe's magic. When you have drunk her potion, draw your sword and threaten to kill her. It's the only way she will agree to turn your crewmates back into men."

Odysseus frowned at the plant. "That's moly – it's poisonous!"

The Adventures of Odysseus

Hermes laughed. "I'm not trying to trick you. When given to you by a god, it will not harm you. Eat it!"

Odysseus paused, but he didn't have much choice. He took the plant and chewed it quickly. It tasted bitter and he nearly spat it out.

"Good." Smiled Hermes, his eyes twinkling. "Now, remember, drink her potion as if all is normal. Then threaten to kill her. You'll have to be convincing. Good luck and farewell!" With a merry wave, he leaped into the air and was gone in the blink of an eye.

The sweet sound of a woman singing echoed through the woods as Odysseus neared a beautiful house with a large pigsty outside. He tried not to wonder which of his men were the pigs currently rooting around in the mud. The woman who greeted him was tall and stunningly beautiful, with a cascade of ginger hair and deep green eyes which flashed when she saw him. "Come inside, stranger, and rest your tired legs. You must be lost to be out walking in the middle of the night!"

Odysseus smiled and asked, "Do you often sing in the night?"

She nodded, "If I can't sleep, it soothes me."

She led him inside and gave him a deep cup into which she poured a sweet-smelling drink.

"Is that honey mixed with wine?" Asked Odysseus.

Circe nodded and smiled, showing sharp teeth. "Enjoy."

Odysseus drank deeply from the cup. It was the most delicious thing he had ever tasted. Trusting to Hermes' gift, he drank more and more until the cup was empty. "Is there any more?" He asked holding the cup out to Circe.

She looked at it, then back at him, dumbfounded. "How…? How are you doing this?" She asked, her voice trembling slightly.

Odysseus smiled grimly and then stood, drawing his sword with a ring of metal on metal. With a small scream, Circe leaped from her chair and tried to run, but he grabbed her cloak and pulled her back. Odysseus slammed her against the wall and held her there with one hand, his sword at her throat.

"You have taken some of my friends – release them. Swear that you will change them back into men or I will end your life right here!" He roared.

Her bright green eyes were wide with terror. She gulped and then nodded.

"I swear by the waters of the River Styx, the river of the Underworld, that I shall do what you ask, without deceit."

Satisfied, Odysseus kept his sword ready while she hurried through to the next room and found a large bottle containing some oil. They then went out to the pigsty, and he watched her carefully as she went around to some of the pigs and rubbed the oil over them. Then she stood back and cried aloud in a language he did not understand. The pigs coated in oil began to glow. Their legs lengthened, their ears and snouts shrunk, and within seconds Odysseus' crewmates were standing there, staring around at the other pigs.

"Come!" Odysseus called, throwing a dirty look at Circe. "We must be away from here. Wherever here is." Then he had an idea. Pointing his sword at the witch again, he bellowed. "Where are we? Which way is Ithaca?"

Circe shook with terror at the sight of the weapon but managed to speak through shaking lips. "I don't know how you can get home, but there is a man near here who can help you. But the route is not for the faint-hearted."

Odysseus scowled at her. "I am not afraid. Who is this man?"

"Tiresias the Seer."

Odysseus frowned. "Tiresias died many years ago."

Circe nodded. "A day's voyage to the night will bring you to a deep cave. It is an entrance to the Underworld. There you can find Tiresias' shade and learn your route home."

Odysseus sighed and looked up at the sky. He knew that she could not be lying, for she had sworn an oath on the waters of the River Styx. Staring up at the stars, he whispered, "What more trials have you got for me, oh gods! Very well. We shall sail to the Underworld."

CHAPTER 4

Odysseus in the Underworld

Eurylochus could not believe his eyes when he saw Odysseus returning the next morning, leading all seven men safely back. He then saw that the hero had brought something else with him. Polites was leading a great, black male goat with curly horns.

"My lord!" Cried Eurylochus. "How did you do it? How did you save our men?"

Odysseus scowled at him. "I did what any leader would do, Eurylochus. I put my men's safety above my own." He elbowed past him and boarded the ship. "We sail north!" He called to the crew, who cheered as their friends also climbed back on board. Eurylochus scrambled to follow them.

"Is Ithaca to the north, then?" He asked hopefully. Odysseus did not answer immediately.

"No, but we must go north regardless. Then I will discover our way home." Confused, Eurylochus stepped before Odysseus and looked him straight in the eye.

"Odysseus, I doubted you before and I am sorry. It doesn't matter what lies to the north, I will not leave your side again."

"No!" Snapped Odysseus. Then he softened his tone and laid a hand on Eurylochus' shoulder. "No, my friend. I dare not take anyone with me. This is a task I must complete alone."

"Why?" Asked Eurylochus. "What is so dreadful that you, oh great king of Ithaca, seem afraid?"

"The witch Circe told me many things," explained Odysseus. "Only Tiresias, the blind man granted the gift of prophecy by the gods, can tell us how to get home. But he died many years ago. Therefore, we must sail to the mouth of the River Styx, the black river which flows around the Underworld. There I can call Tiresias' shade, his spirit, and ask him where we need to go."

Eurylochus went as pale as if he had already seen a ghost. He clutched the side of the ship and gasped. "Are you mad?"

Odysseus shook his head. "No, just desperate."

The sky darkened steadily as they sailed north, before them they could see a long strip of coastline that barred their path. In the center, they could see a huge, shadowy cave. As they came nearer, they saw that it was far larger than even the cave of Polyphemus the cyclops. It was so huge that their ship could sail inside. Out of the cave, there flowed a dark stream of water, as black as ink. Odysseus looked around at his men as they tied up the sail and prepared the oars. Every man looked pale and shaky. Trying to keep his own voice calm, he called to them. "My friends, we are sailing towards the Underworld. But today is not your day to enter that dark realm. I alone will step foot on its shores. Then, we shall finally know how we can return home to Ithaca!"

The mention of their homeland seemed to cheer his men's hearts a little, and with jaws set and eyes downward, they heaved on the oars and rowed forward into the huge cave.

It was as dark as night inside. Odysseus took a single torch, his sword, and the black sheep, and leaped down onto the black soil of the Underworld. Immediately he felt a cold chill as the air seemed to catch in his lungs.

He strode forward a few steps and planted the torch in the ground. A pale mist hung in the air so that although he could hear the water lapping against the shore behind him, the ship was already invisible to him. He began to dig a hole with his sword, scraping away the earth with his sword until he had a small, square trench about a hand's width deep and a foot wide. Grabbing the black ram, which had been cowering nearby, he called out into the dark, cloying mist. "Shades of the Underworld! Hear me! I must speak with Tiresias, the blind prophet of Thebes! Bring him forth!" And with that, he killed the ram and poured its blood into the trench he had dug.

Whispers came echoing out of the fog so that he had no clear idea from which direction they came. His heart was in his mouth, his hair seemed to stand on end. Never in his whole life had Odysseus known terror such as this. Shadowy hands and pale, glowing eyes seemed to float toward him out of the darkness. Then the mist formed into a distinct shape. He recognized the noble face and broad shoulders of Achilles, the great warrior whose death at the hands of Paris had nearly doomed the Greeks to despair and defeat at Troy. Tears welled up in Odysseus' eyes. "Achilles! Speak with me! Help me!"

The shade of Achilles knelt down on the black soil and scooped some of the blood into his mouth. Rising to his feet again, Odysseus heard his voice as though through deep water.

"My old friend. What are you doing here? Surely you cannot also be dead? Tell me that Troy fell and that you have made it safely home!"

Odysseus shook his head, sadly. "We took Troy, Achilles, but I have not made it home yet. You can be happy though, for your name and the tales of your great deeds shall be sung in every hall in Greece!"

Achilles laughed a hollow, sad laugh. "That means nothing to me now, wily Odysseus. I would rather be a slave in a farmer's hut than the king of all these unquiet dead souls. Honor and glory mean nothing here."

Odysseus wept at his friend's words, but he had a mission to complete. "My friend, I must speak with Tiresias. Can you find him and bring him to me? He alone can help me return home."

Achilles nodded and turned away, leaving Odysseus apparently alone in the mist. He shivered not just be with cold, but also a quiet terror: He could sense other spirits moving around him. Faces loomed out of the darkness like clouds and then dispersed as the air shifted. Some were total strangers to him, but some he knew. He saw Philoetius, the young warrior who was the first to die at Troy; the great form of mighty Ajax brought further tears to his eyes. Suddenly another familiar face appeared before him. "Agamemnon!" He whispered, his voice catching in his throat. "Surely you cannot be dead as well?! After we did what no one thought possible and took Troy? How cruel is fate?" The ghost of Agamemnon stared at Odysseus forlornly and then at the trench of blood. Odysseus shook his head. "I'm sorry, my friend. I must save this blood for Tiresias; only he can tell me how to get home!"

Hours seemed to pass in that lifeless void before the pale shade of Achilles returned, leading the ghost of an old man with a bandage over his eyes. The hero's shade helped the other kneel down and drink from the trench. Rising to his feet again, Tiresias turned his unseeing face to Odysseus. "Ask me what you have come to ask, king of Ithaca."

Odysseus took a deep breath and said, "What must I do to bring my men safely home?"

Tiresias shook his head. "You ask the impossible. Your men will never return to Ithaca."

Odysseus shook with rage. "I promised them that I would do so. You cannot stop me!"

"I can't," agreed the shade of the seer, "but the gods can. You have many more trials before you, cunning Odysseus. You must pass by the Sirens but beware of their sweet music. Any man who hears it falls under their spell. Then you must enter the narrow Straits of Darkness. There dwell Charybdis and Scylla. One is a great whirlpool, the other hangs down from the cliffs high above. Neither
can be fought, but you must pass by both. Then you shall come to the island of Helios, the sun-titan. If you can survive there without harming his cattle for a full moon's cycle, then you shall be able to sail homewards."

Odysseus stared at the old seer, who was turning to leave. "Why?" He asked, half-angry, half-terrified. "What have I done wrong to deserve such punishment?"

The ghost of the old man turned and smiled a cruel, mocking smile. "What have you done? Did you not trick Protesilaus into stepping foot on Ilium's shores first instead of you? Did you not betray Philoctetes? Did you not dishonor your friend Ajax? Did you not insult Poseidon by blinding his son, Polyphemus? You have achieved many great things, Odysseus, cunning Odysseus, wily, clever, resourceful Odysseus, king of Ithaca, builder of the Wooden Horse, the man who conquered Troy. But you have done it through the misery and pain of countless others. You have done what all men do: You have written your own destiny. You have sown your crops of glory and now must reap the fruits of your troubles. You shall have glory. You have already gained great riches. Your name shall be remembered forever. But this all comes at a price, Odysseus. The price of suffering."

And so, Tiresias turned away and disappeared into the ice-cold fog, still laughing faintly. Odysseus stared after him, his mouth dry and his limbs shaking with fear and rage. "I will not lose a single man more." He swore to himself. "I will change my destiny. I will!"

CHAPTER 5

The Sirens, Scylla, and Charybdis

>>>>·<<<<

The first warm rays of sunlight after the cold, inky blackness of the Underworld were as refreshing and welcome as a long drink of cold water after days spent in a desert. Every man on Odysseus' ship breathed a sigh of relief as the great cave disappeared over the horizon behind them. They were not rowing, just simply letting the wind blow them onward. Odysseus knew in his heart that they were going the right way. He had not told any of his men what the shade of Tiresias the blind prophet had said. He knew that they would be terrified at the news of the monsters and enraged at the idea of never getting home. He could hardly believe what the old man had said and kept telling himself that he could save his men.

Many days passed without sight of land. Odysseus often wondered why they had not seen even one other ship in all their time at sea. He had lost track of how long it was since they had set sail from Troy. It was almost as though the fog and the winds had taken them beyond the borders of the known world and into a place of terror and lost hope. Shaking himself slightly to rid his mind of the doubtful thoughts, he called up to Amphidamas, who was sitting high atop the mast, craning his neck this way and that, desperately searching for land. Suddenly, he pointed at something on the horizon. "Land! Or at least, a small island."

Odysseus' mind raced. Tiresias had told him that first, they must pass by the Sirens and that their music would lead his men to their deaths. He had no idea what Sirens were but found himself strangely curious to hear what their song sounded like. He ordered Eurylochus to help him soften a great ball of wax. They then stuffed the wax into the men's ears, and bound strips of cloth over them as well, so that they could not hear anything.

"Now, Eurylochus, tie me to the mast. There will be monsters ahead whose song will enter me, and I will order you to release me. Stuff your own ears with wax and ignore me. Do not do anything but row until we have passed the island by, and the sun is setting. Then it should be safe." Eurylochus clearly had his doubts but dared not argue. The trip to the Underworld seemed to have quietened his sharp tongue.

The men went to their oars and silently rowed forwards, pushing the ship on faster. As the small island got nearer, Odysseus heard the gentle strums of a harp wafting over the waves before him. It was like drops of honey falling into his ears. He longed to hear more. Then, he saw them. The Sirens were not monsters at all! They were women.

Such beautiful women as he had never seen before. Yes, they had wings coming out of their shoulders; yes, their eyes were grey as thunder clouds and their hair as dark as night; yes, he could see countless bones of men lying around them. But they sang so beautifully that nothing else mattered except that he kept listening.

> "Come join us, handsome sailor!
> Come rest your weary head.
> Let the wind and waves go wandering,
> Join us and sing instead.
> The sun is hot, the sea is wide,
> Your ship is never still.
> Our isle is fair, our song is sweet,
> Your desires we shall fulfill!"

As the ship sailed past, Odysseus strained at the ropes with all his might. He roared at his men to let him loose; he shouted, kicked, and wriggled, but the ropes held tight. The island of the Sirens slipped behind them until it was just a spot on the horizon. As the memory of the music faded, Odysseus found his head clearing. The wild thoughts of leaping ashore were gone and he remembered Tiresias' warning. He felt strangely drained, and when Eurylochus finally cleared his own ears of wax and untied him, he slipped to the floor as weak and shaky as if he had just run a mile.

The next day dawned, and Amphidamas, back up atop the mast called down again.

"Land, or at least I think it is! It looks like another great cave."

Odysseus' heart sank. "No more caves!" He thought.

But as they sailed further, they could see that Amphidamas was wrong. There was land ahead, or rather one great chunk of land to the left, and a huge island to the right. Between them was a narrow gap, perhaps a hundred feet across, and the cliffs on either side were so high that the strait between them was full of gloom and shadow. Remembering the words of Tiresias, Odysseus knew he had a choice to make. The Straits of Darkness were the home of two undefeatable monsters: Scylla and Charybdis. Scylla lived high up on the cliffs and could not be fought but would still kill many of his men. Charybdis, according to Tiresias, was a great whirlpool. "There is no real choice here." Muttered Odysseus. "Charybdis will swallow this ship whole and all of us on it. But if we sail through quickly, only a few of us will be killed by Scylla." He shook his head sadly. "I will get as many of my men home as I can. But some will have to die so that the others can live."

As they entered the Straits, Amphidamas shouted, "There is a strong current pulling us through, it seems to lead us to the right-hand side!"

"Then we row to the left!" Cried Odysseus. "Quickly! Every man row as hard as you can!"

Amphidamas slid down the mast like a squirrel and took up an oar. Odysseus grabbed the tiller and Polites, and the helmsman sat next to Eurylochus and pulled as hard as he could.

"Row!" Odysseus shouted, staring up at the cliffs above them. Away to the right, he could see the waves going round and round in a circle. A great rushing and sucking noise came to his ears. The ship plunged to the right, and he heaved the tiller over, steering them away from Charybdis. "Row!" He bellowed. "Row! Your lives depend on it!"

Slowly, ever so slowly they inched away from the whirlpool and on through the Straits. But there was no time to relax. Without warning, something dived down from the cliffs above and grabbed Polites. Odysseus had a second's glimpse of a great head on a long neck like a snake, saw a mouth full of foot-long teeth, and then it was gone, taking Polites with it. The men cried with rage and fear, and several reached for their weapons. "No!" Odysseus roared. "Keep rowing! There is no fighting such a monster. Row!"

Scylla's head plucked another man, Lycaon, from the bench behind Amphidamas as though he were nothing but a grape on a plate. The man screamed and then was lost to the dark cliffs above. The men ducked their heads over their oars and heaved with all their might. Finally, they saw light ahead of them as the Straits opened and the wind filled their sails again. With the danger behind them, Eurylochus abandoned his oar and stomped over to face Odysseus.

"You knew!" He shouted. "You knew what faced us back there!"

Odysseus nodded but said nothing.

Eurylochus was shaking with rage. "You could have saved Polites and Lycaon. We could have been ready to fight that thing, whatever it was!"

"There was no fighting such a creature." Odysseus' voice was surprisingly calm. "Our only chance was all to row as hard as we could. I steered us away from the whirlpool, Charybdis, otherwise, we would all be dead now."

Eurylochus' eyes blazed. "You even know what these things are called?! Did Tiresias tell you all this? What more awaits us, Odysseus? Tell us!"

Odysseus shook his head. "We are nearly home. You must trust me."

"Trust you? How can we trust you when you won't share what you know?" Roared Eurylochus.

"Because I am your leader and I have promised to get you all home. I saved our men from the witch Circe; I got us out of the cyclops' cave; I will get as many of us back to Ithaca as I can!"

Eurylochus shook his head. "A leader is nothing without his crew. We are a team, Odysseus, or we used to be. You always shared your plans with us but now you keep everything a secret. That is no way to lead."

Odysseus scowled and turned away, staring at the horizon, wondering how long before they would reach the island of Helios the sun-titan, and face their last trial.

I hope you enjoy the book. Please kindly leave a review.

CHAPTER 6

The Island of Helios

As the island rose out of the horizon ahead of them, Odysseus' heart sank. His men were all overjoyed to see it, for islands meant water, fresh food, and possibly even people. But Odysseus knew that this island meant only fresh challenges. He was tired of it all. The constant danger and fear that they had endured since leaving Troy pressed down on him like a weight. As the island loomed over them, dark with trees, Odysseus raised his eyes to the sky. "Gods of Olympus," he prayed, "hear me. Have we not suffered enough? Let me and my men survive and reach Ithaca." He turned away from the island to order his men to prepare to go ashore when what he saw behind them made his heart sink even further. Storm clouds loomed behind them. The wind was blowing them straight for the island. His men cheered at what they thought was a good sign, but Odysseus bowed his head, remembering the words of Tiresias, the blind prophet he had met in the Underworld.

Clenching his fists, he turned to his men. "Listen all of you! When I went to the Underworld, I was warned about this island by Tiresias. It belongs to Helios, the titan whose chariot pulls the sun across the sky. There we shall find cattle, but they are not to be touched, for they are sacred to Helios. Please, listen to me, for I do not want to lose one more man on this journey."

Every man looked at each other, scared, but Eurylochus nodded his head and said, "Thank you, Odysseus, thank you for sharing what you know with us. Let's get off this island as soon as possible!"

They managed to land their ship safely but as the storm crashed against the island, they were forced to go further inland, where they found refuge under the trees. The next day the storm clouds had disappeared, but the wind was still just as strong. So strong, in fact, that there was no chance of their sailing away from the island. Memories of their struggles at Aulis, what seemed a lifetime ago, came back to Odysseus. The goddess Artemis, angry at Agamemnon, had sent a constant wind to stop the Greek fleet from sailing to Troy. Only with the sacrifice of his own daughter had the goddess let them go.

Striking out across the island to find food, they soon found the cattle Tiresias had told them about. The cows were, indeed, beautiful, with golden horns and pure white coats, all except for the bull, which was black as coal. Remembering the dire warning of the blind prophet, they steered clear of the herd and continued their search for other animals, berries, nuts, and fruit. But they found nothing. The only thing to be found was the grass the cows ate, and the cows themselves. Odysseus ordered his men to set traps, and they spent hours by the shore, hoping to catch some fish to eat. They had some supplies, and the sea brought them the occasional fish, which they shared gladly. But hunger soon began to gnaw at them.

Each night, Odysseus watched the moon rise in the sky. Each night, it grew a little more, having been just a thin sliver when they had first arrived. Even as it came to the full, the wind still had not stopped blowing. Eurylochus was starting to grumble. "When will this wind stop? What have we done to deserve this?" Odysseus didn't have an answer for him, so ignored him. This seemed to make Eurylochus even angrier. "Why should we listen to an old, dead prophet anyway?" He asked. "What if he was wrong?"

Odysseus turned on him, equally angry. "Tiresias was right about the Sirens, and he was right about Scylla and Charybdis. Why would he be wrong this time?"

Eurylochus had no answer to this either, so just glowered and then turned away.

The days wore on, and the men started to fight amongst each other. Everyone accused the others of hiding food from the rest. Odysseus went from one man to the next, trying to calm them, trying to reassure them that the wind must let up soon.

"We can get through this only if we stick together." He said to each man. "We have survived through so much already; we can survive this!"

Eurylochus was not so positive. "Artemis only stopped the wind at Aulis when King Agamemnon sacrificed his dearest daughter!" He spat angrily. "What do we have to give in return for our freedom?!"

As the third week of their captivity on the island came to an end, even Odysseus had to admit that things were looking desperate for them. Hardly any of them had the strength left to go fishing or search the woods for something they could eat. Most of them just lay in the makeshift shelter they had built. One day, however, Eurylochus came to Odysseus and addressed him before the rest of the crew. "We have only one choice, Odysseus. We must kill one of those cows. There are so many of them wandering over this island, I doubt the sun-titan Helios will miss just one!"

Odysseus stared at him. "Do you not remember the warning of Tiresias? To touch those cattle means death!"

"To leave them alone means death too!" Shouted Eurylochus, pushing Odysseus roughly.

Growling, Odysseus shoved him back, knocking him against a tree. "Listen to me!" He said firmly, looking at all the men, not just Eurylochus. "I am just as hungry as any of you. But the prophet was not wrong about the Sirens or the Straits of Darkness. I have led you well since we left Troy and although we have lost friends along the way, it is still my aim to bring all of you home safely. Do not touch the cattle, the wind must stop soon!"

That night, Eurylochus woke all of the men except Odysseus. "Do you really believe him?" He asked in a whisper. "He did not tell us about Scylla and Charybdis before, and we lost two good men. He kept the secret of the bag of winds from us, and that was what started all this bad luck for us. Who knows what other secrets the blind prophet told him. I say we take our chances and feast on one of those cattle. I'd rather die quickly with a full belly than die slowly of starvation!"

Every man agreed with him, and so they crept away from the shelter and found one of the beautiful, snow-white cows. It did not fear them, simply watched as Eurylochus strode forward and killed it with a single blow with his sword.

Odysseus woke to the delicious smell of beef cooking on a wood fire. His mouth watering, it took a few moments before he realized what this meant. Leaping to his feet, he cried, "You fools! You have doomed us!" But his crew were all too happy enjoying the meat to care. Odysseus refused to touch even a mouthful. He kept looking at the sky, as though expecting to see Helios himself riding down on his chariot to crush them all underfoot. Even as he looked, the clouds seemed to stop moving, and then start going back the way they had come. The wind had changed.

"Ha!" Laughed Eurylochus through a mouthful of beef. "I knew it! The cow was the sacrifice necessary. Now we can go home!"

There was a raucous cheer and the men packed up the rest of the meat. They all ran aboard the ship and set sail, Odysseus silent and sad, standing at the rear.

The island was just falling from sight behind them when a great wave slapped against the side of the boat. Then another smacked against the other side. Glancing around in sudden fear, Eurylochus cried aloud as he looked upwards. All turned their eyes skywards to see a huge, black storm cloud blossoming above them as if from nowhere. Odysseus said nothing as tears fell from his eyes. The sea tossed them this way and that, every man desperately clinging to ropes, trying to stay on board. Thunder boomed overhead and the clouds flashed brightly against black as lightning flickered across them. Then a single fork of lightning hurtled down from the sky and struck the mast of the ship. It exploded into a thousand pieces and the ship split in two. All were hurled into the water as more lightning bolts zoomed down like burning arrows. Odysseus managed to grab hold of a large piece of wood that had been part of the mast's crossbeam. Looking around, he could not see a single man alive in the violently churning sea. More tears mixed with salt water as he clung to the wooden beam. He was alone. Completely alone.

CHAPTER 7

Calypso

Odysseus had no idea how long he clung to that wooden beam as the waves knocked him back and forth. It might have been four days; it might have been forty. All he knew was that he had to keep going. As another day dawned, he finally saw an island ahead of him. Using the last of his strength, he swam desperately to shore and dragged himself up the beach, silently thanking the gods for his safe delivery. Then he fell unconscious, exhausted beyond anything he had ever known.

He was awoken by the most beautiful woman he had ever seen. Her eyes might well have been stars in the night of her black hair, which fell to her hips. She and her maids helped Odysseus to the cave in which they dwelt. It was richly decorated with paintings and well-made seats and tables.

"Rest here, friend." Said his hostess, as she brought him to a small alcove in the rock where a bed had been made ready for him, with soft sheets, warm blankets, and a curtain that she closed around him, giving him privacy. He murmured his thanks and fell asleep almost immediately, as his first night on this island loomed over them.

The next day he woke refreshed as though he had slept for weeks, not for hours. He stood and stretched, then found fresh clothes hanging over a chair ready for him. He changed and swept the curtain aside to feel the salt breeze from the sea wafting through the cave's mouth.

"Good morning!" Called several of the women going around their business.

"Good morning!" He returned the greeting, feeling a smile stretching his face, his skin was still sore from his many days at the mercy of the open waves. Whatever they were cooking by the fire smelt good, so he joined his hostess at the table. The warmth of the flames was nothing compared to the warmth of her smile, however. "Welcome to Ogygia." She grinned. "I am Calypso, and you have nothing to fear here, Odysseus."

The hero frowned. "How do you know who I am?"

"You talked a lot in your sleep, Odysseus. You have suffered greatly. Eat, drink, rest, and let time ease the pain from your bones." She clapped her hands and the maids brought up freshly cooked fish, as well as cheese and sweet fruits. While they ate, the gentle rush and hiss of the waves on the rocks outside provided a calming music to their breakfast. All day, Calypso asked Odysseus many questions about the war at Troy. She was immensely interested in everything but found the number of names of the various heroes hard to follow at times. "We get visitors so rarely here," she sighed. "The world outside seems to go by so fast."

"Why not take a ship and visit other islands?" Asked Odysseus curiously.

Calypso laughed and shook her beautiful head. "Leave Ogygia? Never! I have everything I could ever want here."

The sun was sinking into the sea, casting a red light across the sky, ending Odysseus' second day on the island.

On the third day, Odysseus told her tales of his journey from Troy. Calypso was a very good audience: her hands were over her mouth at his description of the monster Scylla; she laughed at his calling himself "Nobody" in the cyclops' cave; and she held his hand tightly as he told of the last, fateful month on the island of Helios. By this point, Odysseus was weeping openly. He was having trouble remembering his crewmen's names, and this made him even sadder. "It was barely a week ago that I lost them all!" He cried. "How can I forget them so easily?"

"Time heals all wounds, dear Odysseus." His hostess said soothingly. "Sleep now, and let your troubles fall away."

On the fourth day, Calypso led him on a tour of the island. Odysseus was astonished to see the variety of wild fruits and crops which seemed to grow of their own accord. Everything from dates and olives to wheat and barley. Sheep clustered around them, as tame as dogs, and yet there was no sign of wolves or any other predator. "It seems to be a paradise." He murmured to himself, as he and Calypso watched the sun setting again in the wine-dark sea. "Why indeed would anyone want to leave here?" But even as he said this and took another sip of wine, his heart began to ache in his chest.

Odysseus spent the fifth day on the island helping the maids catch fish in the shallow waters of the wide lagoon on the island's south side. Here the water was as clear and blue as the sky above. The women drew a net across the water, chasing the fish towards Odysseus and a couple of others, who stood ready with spears to skewer what they could. Laughing, Odysseus heaved a great sea bass onto the sand and glanced up the beach to see Calypso watching him, a small smile twisting her lips. Something about that look made him uneasy, and suddenly the ache in his chest he had felt the previous evening returned stronger than before. Turning away from the island, he stared out to sea, a single name echoing through his mind, although he could not quite catch it on his tongue.

The next morning, Odysseus awoke from a night of disturbed sleep. All night he had been haunted by the face of a beautiful woman whom he chased through the empty hallways of a great house. He could never quite catch up to her. As he sat up a name burst from his lips and tears flooded down his cheeks. "Penelope!" The pain in his heart redoubled and now he knew why. He must get home to Ithaca, to his dear wife Penelope. Calypso's face grew grave as he spoke to her of his desire to leave. "No one leaves my island, Odysseus." She said firmly. "You have been here too long, she will not want you back."

Odysseus snorted. "My wife is true to me, Calypso. Six days on this island means nothing to me. I will return home."

"Enough of this!" A firm voice echoed from the cave mouth. Both of them turned to see a young man with golden skin striding towards them. Odysseus recognized him. "Hermes! Messenger of the gods!" He bowed, and Calypso scowled.

"I have given this man a home after all you gods have chased him around the sea, giving him nothing but abuse and pain. Let him stay here!"

Hermes frowned. "Daughter of Atlas, you know that he is not destined to end his days on Ogygia. You have shown him great kindness and healed his wounds, but neither you nor I can stop the tides of fate. Let him go!"

Calypso bowed her head sadly and Hermes turned to Odysseus. "It has been a while since we last saw each other, great Odysseus. Poseidon, the god of the sea, has ended his revenge against you for blinding his son, Polyphemus. You must hurry, for time is strangely short."

Odysseus stared at the god, dumbfounded. "What do you mean, time is short?"

Hermes glared angrily at Calypso. "You never told him?! Time works differently here on Ogygia: For every day that passes here a year passes in the world outside."

The hero's jaw dropped; he could scarcely believe it. Meanwhile, Hermes continued speaking.

"You have been away from home for far longer than you thought, Odysseus. But now all will be well. Build a raft and sail away without fear. You shall be met by a ship from Phaeacia, they are the best sailors in the world. They shall take you home. Farewell, we shall not see each other again."

With a wave of his hand, Hermes flew out of the cave. Odysseus collected tools, rope, and an axe from the back of the cave and set to work. He put down small trees, tied them together with rope, and made a small mast. Calypso's maids brought him a great sheet for the sail, and Calypso herself helped him load baskets of bread, fruit, and sacks of wine onto the raft, by which point the sun had set and the moon was already rising, bringing Odysseus' sixth day on Ogygia to a close.

As the seventh day dawned, Odysseus was already awake. He sprang out of bed to find Calypso already standing, watching the sunrise. A single tear rolled down her cheek as they said their farewells.

"You don't have to go, you know." She said, quietly. "I can make you immortal. We could live here on my island forever. Out there, you shall grow old and weak, and someday you shall die."

"Thank you, Calypso, but no." Said Odysseus. "I am sorry that I cannot stay, but I have another life beyond these shores. All my suffering has taught me many things, but one thing above all: It is the unknown which defines us, and how we meet it when it comes. I cannot live here, knowing that every day will be the same for eternity." She nodded, her sadness stopping all words. Having heaved the raft out into the shallows, Odysseus sailed away without a second glance. "Seven days, no seven years." He whispered. "And ten years already away at Troy. Will Penelope even recognize me after so long a time? And my son, he must be nearly a man!" His heart ached still, but his spirit rose as the waves flew beneath him and Ogygia sank into the horizon.

As the sun passed over him and down towards the horizon again, he cried with joy as a sail crested the waves ahead of him, and he saw a great ship coming towards him. Hermes' promise had come true.

"Where have you come from?" Called the Phaeacian captain as his men helped Odysseus onboard. "And where are you going to?"

Odysseus laughed. "The tale of my journey would make an epic poem! As for where I am going, I am Odysseus, lord of Ithaca, and I am going home."

The captain smiled. "It so happens that we are passing that way ourselves. The gods must love you. Rest your head over there and we'll let you know when it's time to get off."

Weariness seemed to drag Odysseus' shoulders downwards and yawning, he stumbled over to the bed the captain had indicated. His eyes were already closing even as he lay down.

CHAPTER 8

The Suitors

≫≫➤ · ⫷⫷⫷

Odysseus awoke, expecting to see the Phaeacian captain shaking him awake. To his horror, he found himself lying on yet another beach. He leaped to his feet and stared out at the sea. There was no ship in sight. "Damn you Phaeacians!" He roared. "Where have you left me now?" He heard footsteps behind him and turned quickly to find himself staring into the face of a man he thought he knew but could not quite remember. "Stranger," said the man, "I am Eumaeus the swineherd. You are alive, but only just. Do not be afraid, my house is near and there you may stay while you recover."

With difficulty, the swineherd helped Odysseus stagger up the narrow path to his house. There, Eumaeus gave Odysseus a fresh cloak and a big plate of cheese, meat, and bread, with a cup of wine to wash it down. Only when he was finished, did Eumaeus ask him, "Who are you, stranger? How did you come to wash up on Ithaca?" Odysseus could barely believe his ears. But his memory told him it was true – he knew this man and knew that he could not be lying. He was home at last!

Smiling broadly, he replied, "Eumaeus, you know me. Have I changed so much since I left for Troy? I am Odysseus, son of Laertes!"

Eumaeus' face went white with shock, then his eyes widened, and recognized his king. Falling to his knees he kissed Odysseus' hands, crying happy tears. "Lord!" He cried, "Lord, pardon my not recognizing you, but it has been twenty years since you left, and you have changed so much!"

Odysseus' jaw dropped. "Twenty years?" He looked down at his hands, felt his face, and found that they were indeed aged with time and hardship. "What cruel magic is this?" He whispered. "Ten years at war, ten years lost at sea. Time flowed by like some evil river." Looking at his reflection in the water basin, he saw that his hair and beard were also tinged with grey. "Half my life has been lost to that ill-fated war at Troy. My son must now be a man." He muttered miserably. But then he straightened up and turned to face the swineherd. "But I am home now, and I will lose no more time!"

He would have rushed out the door at that moment, had Eumaeus not grabbed him by the arm.

"Lord, forgive me, but you must be careful!" Cried the loyal swineherd. "As you have been gone so long, lords from Ithaca and beyond have come to contest for Queen Penelope's hand in marriage and become king themselves! They are a disrespectful lot. By all rights, they should have gone to Icarius her father, but they want your land as well. So, they lie around your house, drinking, and eating, waiting for her to choose a new husband from among them."

Clenching his fists, Odysseus growled. "How dare they?!" But then he frowned. "I must be cautious. So many things will have changed since I left. I cannot know now whom I can trust, except for you, dear Eumaeus. I shall disguise myself as a beggar and sneak into the palace. But you must be ready to help me when I need you."

Eumaeus nodded. "I go there nearly every day as I herd the pigs. I shall be ready when you call."

Odysseus took the cloak Eumaeus had given him and rolled it and himself in the dirt. He rubbed earth into his face, hair, and beard, and made a walking stick out of a branch. Then he borrowed a satchel from Eumaeus to complete the disguise of a wandering beggar. Having thus hidden his identity, he made his way up the paths he remembered so well to his own palace. The evening was closing in as he arrived, and fresh tears rolled down his cheeks as he saw his old home looming out of the dusk. Inside he could hear raucous singing. Grinding his teeth, he bent his back over his walking stick and hobbled inside the great doors, not knowing what he would find inside.

A rush of smells and sounds and sights assaulted his senses as he entered the main courtyard, all heartfully familiar and yet strange due to his many years at war and then at sea. He could see the servants, some of whose names he could still remember, going about their work as usual. But between them and around them many men lay about lazily. His temper rose as he saw them shouting at his servants, demanding more wine, more food, or simply lashing out with hand or foot because the hard-working man or woman had dared step too near them.

"Eurymachus!" shouted one of the louts with a thick beard and dark eyebrows. "What game shall we play tonight?"

Eurymachus, a tall, good-looking noble smiled. "Your guess is as good as mine, Antinous. Will lady Penelope finally finish her task and chose us? What is your bet?"

Antinous barked with laughter. "It has been three years since she started her great labor, how long does it take to sew a funeral shroud?"

Odysseus' heart was in his mouth. "Funeral shroud?" he murmured to himself. "Who has died? For whom does my dear wife work at her loom to make a shroud?"

Eurymachus rolled his eyes. "I know, my friend. The ridiculous thing is that Laertes, the father of Odysseus, still lives! Why she feels the need to start sewing now is beyond me!"

Another man raised his voice, "My friends, lord Laertes is old and yet strong, but I think lady Penelope is right to do this final service for her father-in-law before she takes another man's hand."

Antinous threw a cup of wine at the speaker. "Amphinomus, you cotton-headed fool. The only service she should complete is to choose one of us as her new husband. That is all that women is fit for. Ithaca needs a king, and it's about time Penelope stopped her weaving and made up her mind!"

Eurymachus rose and patted Antinous on the shoulder. "Why the hurry, Antinous? I want her to choose a new husband as much as any of you. Why else am I here? But until she decides, we can drink and eat to our hearts' content. The gods know that Odysseus is not going to walk in that door and stop us, so let the woman work and enjoy Odysseus' good wine and food while you wait!"

The other suitors laughed and cheered at this. Odysseus, meanwhile, gripped his staff furiously and glared at the arrogant young nobles who so disrespected his house and family.

It was then that Antinous noticed the beggar for the first time. "Who is this who hobbles into this noble house?" He roared, grabbing another cup of wine from a servant and drinking deeply. "Get out, you little thief – there are no free meals to be had here!"

"Silence, Antinous!" Cried a new voice. All turned to see who had spoken. A young man with a light beard had entered the courtyard. He was tall but well-built, and his eyes were dark and keen. Odysseus knew those eyes, for they had looked out at him from mirrors all his life. For the first time in twenty years, Odysseus saw his son Telemachus and tears fell down his cheeks to see this fine young man, so noble and tall.

Telemachus strode forward and took Odysseus by the arm. "Welcome, stranger. Find a seat and rest. I shall send someone to look after you. Do not worry about these men." He glowered at the suitors. "My father, King Odysseus, is away, but until his return, my mother and I rule here." He turned and addressed the assembled men. "Do not forget that I am the prince of Ithaca, noble lords. This is still my father's house, and my word is the law here." With that, he left.

"That young idiot needs to be taught a lesson." Murmured Eurymachus.

Antinous finished his cup and growled, "I've told you; we should have killed him ages ago. Once he is dead, there is nothing tying Penelope to Odysseus. She will have to choose!"

Amphinomus looked stunned. "Do you want to bring the gods' anger down on us, Antinous? There is no need to murder the young prince. He is still too young to become king. Once his mother remarries, he will not be a threat. I will have no part in such bloodshed."

Eurymachus and Antinous raised their eyebrows at each other, but neither argued further.

Meanwhile, Odysseus, still disguised as a beggar, sat by the fire warming his hands, his heart beating against his ribs like a great drum. If he didn't act soon, he would lose his wife, his son, and his home.

CHAPTER 9

Penelope

Penelope looked carefully out of her window at the courtyard below. She had heard her son Telemachus shouting at the suitors about something, but by the time she had rushed to the window, the commotion had died down again. Down in the courtyard, she could just see Eurymachus, Antinous, and Amphinomus locked in a heated argument. She sighed deeply and stepped back from the window. "Oh, how I hate them all! I wish they would just leave!" She muttered, slumping down into a chair, "Oh, where is Odysseus?" She had lost count of how many times she had asked herself this over the past ten years. Ever since they had heard of the Greeks' victory at Troy, she had been eagerly awaiting her husband's return. But days passed, then weeks, finally years, and she had begun to lose hope. "He will return." She told herself firmly. "And I shall wait for him, no matter how many men come asking for my hand." She shuddered at the thought of marrying any of those drunken swine down in the courtyard.

There came a knock at the door and Melantho, her maid came in. "Do you need anything else tonight, my lady?" She asked politely. She glanced at the long loom that stood along the wall next to the window, the machine Penelope used to sew the funeral shroud for her father-in-law, Laertes. The shroud itself was magnificent, but still only half-finished. "You're making good progress, my lady." She commented. "It will be wonderful once it is done." There was a look in the maid's eyes that Penelope didn't quite like.

"Just remember to bring me a fresh dress for tomorrow, but there's no hurry now." She said, standing up and reaching for her nightgown. Melantho bowed and left. Penelope changed her clothes and then stopped to listen. The noise in the courtyard had quietened down, meaning that all the suitors had gone to bed. She crossed to the loom and began to undo the work she had done that day. She had done this nearly every night since she had begun the shroud. This was why it had taken her so long. She smiled to herself as she pulled more threads away, "Those fools have no idea, and so long as I keep working, they must wait, by which time Odysseus will have come back!"

Her heart leaped as the door opened behind her. Melantho stood there, a dress folded carefully over her arm, her mouth slightly open. "My lady...?" She was staring at the shroud and the threads lying all over the floor – Penelope hadn't had time to tidy them away yet. Thinking fast, Penelope explained, "I wasn't happy with today's work, that's all. I saw a knot in one of the rows and it wouldn't do to leave it like that."

The Adventures of Odysseus

Melantho shook her head slowly. "No, of course not, my lady." She smiled and hung the dress on the hook behind the door. "Goodnight." She said, bowing again. But again, Penelope did not like the look in her eyes. The door closed and Penelope sank onto the bed, her head in her hands. "Surely I can trust my own maid?" She whispered to the silence of the night.

Down in the courtyard, not everyone was asleep. Odysseus the beggar was sitting by the fire, warming himself and washing his tired, dirty feet in a bowl of water, his long, mud-stained tunic tucked up over his knees. He heard light footsteps behind him and twisted around, hand reaching for his walking stick. But it was only an old woman, a servant, carrying a couple of blankets. He recognized her. It was Eurycleia, a servant who had worked in the house since he was a child. She had been still a young woman when first he had known her, but time had worn her beauty away. Penelope had chosen her to be Telemachus' nurse, for she was wise, caring, and loyal. Now she stood there, surveying him in the firelight. "My lord asked me to bring you some blankets and to see if there was anything else you needed." Her old voice was croaky like a frog's, but he could see that her eyes were still sharp and watchful. Odysseus smiled despite himself. "Thank you, I am fine. I have water for my feet, and a warm fire, and will gratefully take those blankets off you." He reached out, but the old woman's keen eyes suddenly widened as she stared at his left leg, on which the firelight glowed brightly. "That scar!" She breathed. "I know that scar!" Odysseus glanced down at his own leg. On the shin of his left leg was a long, jagged scar. As a young man, he had gone boar-hunting in the forests of Ithaca with his father when the boar they were chasing had turned on them. He had been too slow, and the boar's tusks had raked up his leg. He remembered that it had been Eurycleia herself who had sewn up the wound and tended it afterward.

"Odysseus!" She gasped. Odysseus leaped to his feet and clamped his hand over her mouth.

"Be silent, or we shall all be dead!" He whispered. Then more footsteps, these ones firm and loud, echoed in the quiet courtyard behind him.

"What is the meaning of this, beggar?" Demanded Telemachus. "I sent my dearest servant to see to your needs, and you repay my hospitality by attacking her. Give me one good reason why I should not kill you where you stand!"

Odysseus released his hold on the old woman and turned to face his son. "I am your father, Telemachus. I am Odysseus, lord of Ithaca. I have returned and will clean the filth from our house, with your help, if you have inherited my strength as well as my temper!"

Telemachus' jaw dropped. He stared at Odysseus for a long moment, then gave Eurycleia a swift, questioning glance. She nodded. "It is true, dear lord, I swear it. This is your father!"

Half-laughing, half-crying, Telemachus threw himself at Odysseus and hugged him. Odysseus too could not hold back his tears. "We must prepare." He said, "I have a plan."

The next day dawned bright, and Penelope went down into the courtyard to speak with the suitors, as was the custom. She hated this tiresome duty, but she had no choice. They were all waiting for her as she stepped out into the sunlight. Antinous and a few others already had cups of wine in their hands. With a sudden thrill of terror, she saw that Melantho stood by Eurymachus, whispering something to him. Her heart in her mouth, she tried to smile but then Eurymachus stepped forward and her voice died in her throat.

"My friends," he cried, addressing the other suitors, "I have learned of a great deceit! Queen Penelope has not been working hard on the shroud for noble Laertes as she has told us. Every night she undoes much of what she has done. That is why she is not yet finished after three years! Truly she is a cunning schemer to rival even her husband Odysseus!"

He turned to face Penelope. "This ends now, Penelope, you must choose one of us today."

Penelope stood proud and upright, staring around the courtyard at the suitors. Her son, Telemachus, stood by the gates with an old beggar, his face like thunder. Sighing, she nodded. "Noble suitors, lord Eurymachus is right. This ends today."

CHAPTER 10

The Trial of Axes

Every man in the courtyard was silent as they stared up at the beautiful queen, Penelope. She truly was an amazing woman. Not only had she run the kingdom of Ithaca for 20 years while her husband, Odysseus, was away, but she had also successfully deceived all these men for nearly three years – pretending to be making a funeral shroud for her father-in-law, Laertes. In reality, she had been steadily undoing the work each night, so that the progress had been incredibly slow. Thus, she had kept them waiting, while she waited for the true king's return. But she had been betrayed by her maid, Melantho, who had told Eurymachus, one of the suitors, of her scheme. Thankfully, she had also thought of a plan in case Odysseus had not returned before she had completed the shroud. She raised her chin and addressed the assembled suitors. "I have a challenge for you all. My husband had a great bow, the man who can string it and shoot an arrow through the loops of twelve axes shall be named my husband and king of Ithaca." She turned on her heel and left the courtyard.

Servants came, and the axes were set out in a line, a string passed carefully through their loops to prove that the line was straight. Then the great bow was brought forth from the treasury with Odysseus' own quiver of hunting arrows. Meanwhile, the suitors had all begun drinking again, each man convinced that he would be successful. What they did not notice was Eumaeus the swineherd and his friend Philoetius entering the courtyard carrying a large lumpy bundle. They locked all the doors leading off the hall and stood near Telemachus, watching, and waiting.

Each of the suitors tried to string the bow. Their eyes bulged and their knuckles cracked with the effort, but none of them could manage it. Even Eurymachus, who was strong and tall, finally gave up. "It cannot be done!" He cried, "That trickster has deceived us again!" Then Odysseus tossed aside his walking stick, strode forwards, and picked up his old bow. "It can be done by the true king of Ithaca!" He shouted at the amazed men, some staggering to their feet to watch, cups of wine still in hand. Behind the crowd of watchers, Telemachus, Eumaeus, and Philoetius were unpacking the bundle, pulling out shields and swords for the three of them. None of the suitors noticed them, for they were all staring at the old beggar as if spellbound. With amazing speed, Odysseus strung the bow and nocked an arrow to the string. Kneeling, he took careful aim. With a soft *twang*, the arrow flew through all twelve loops and struck the wall on the far side of the courtyard. Every man took a step back, amazed at this old man.

Odysseus rose to his full height and cried. "You drunken dogs! I am Odysseus, lord of Ithaca. I have returned, past monsters, through storms, and even into the Underworld itself. Now, see what happens to those who dishonor my family and try to steal what is mine!" Drawing the bow again, he let fly, sending an arrow straight into the heart of Antinous. Telemachus and the others charged from behind, roaring their battle cries. Some of the suitors tried to fight, but they were all unarmed, and many were too drunk to even stand. Eurymachus reached for one of the axes, but Odysseus shot him through the chest, and he crashed to the ground. Within moments the only men left alive in the courtyard were Odysseus and his three comrades.

Telemachus laughed, dancing around the bodies. "It's over! We are free from these horrible men." Odysseus grabbed him by the shoulder, frowning.

"Death is not something to be happy about, my son. We should get our home cleaned up and bury these men suitably." He turned around quickly as someone behind him screamed. The old nurse, Eurycleia, stood at the doorway to the palace, her hands over her mouth. Leaping up the steps, Odysseus turned her away from the horrible sight. "Don't be afraid, dear nurse." He said kindly. "We shall clean this. You must go up to lady Penelope and tell her that her husband has returned." She nodded, a small smile creasing her wrinkly skin.

Penelope sat on the bed in her room with the windows closed, horrified at the sounds of battle and death echoing up from the courtyard. She had not expected any of the suitors to be able to string the bow, because it had been made especially for her husband, who was a greater, stronger man than any of them. But she had not expected them all to start fighting amongst themselves. She shuddered to think of all the blood staining the courtyard. "But perhaps it is better this way." She said to herself. "If they all fight, perhaps they will leave me in peace." A knock at the door made her jump slightly.

"Come in!"

Old Eurycleia entered, her old pale face creased with a broad smile. "My lady!" She cried. "The most wonderful thing has happened."

Penelope nodded. "I have heard the shouts and noises of battle – how many of those evil suitors lie dead?"

"All of them, my lady, but that is not the best thing I have to tell you. Lord Odysseus has returned! It was he who strung the great bow and with it, he, Telemachus, and two others slew all the suitors!"

Penelope felt her jaw drop. Her heart pounded against her ribs and tears crept down her cheeks. But then her mind raced. "I don't believe it." She said, shaking slightly, "I cannot believe it." She thought for a moment. Then her eyes fell on the bed Odysseus had built himself. He had made it out of a tree that had grown by the palace, and it was part of the bedroom itself, holding up one corner of the roof. She had an idea. Pulling a cloak around her shoulders, she went down to the courtyard where she found the beggar helping Eumaeus, Telemachus, and Philoetius carrying the bodies outside the palace gates. Waving the others away, she stood before the beggar.

Odysseus stood and watched his dear wife, who was staring at him, her eyes narrowed with suspicion.

"So, you are the man who claims to be Odysseus." She said slowly. "Then welcome, my husband. I shall order the servants to bring our bed downstairs so that we can spend our first night together under the stars, as we did when we were first married."

Odysseus laughed out loud when he heard this, "My lady Penelope, you are an amazing woman! Herakles himself could not lift that bed from where it sits without bringing the whole room crashing down around him. When I built that bed, all those years ago, I said to you: Around this bed, we shall build our world."

Tears flooded down Penelope's cheeks as she threw herself at her husband. They embraced and held each other close, after twenty long, painful years apart. Finally, Odysseus found the strength to speak again. "I am sorry that I have been so long away. The gods, the winds, and the waves would not allow it, but now I have returned to you, and I swear that I shall never leave your side again."

10-MINUTE STORY SERIES

For 9-12years old

MYTHOLOGY

The Iliad & The Odyssey

Gods, Heroes & Monsters

Egypt, Mesopotamia & Norse

And more are coming soon ....

Scan the QR Code to get a Free e-book straight to your email! You will always catch all newly released series.

GLOSSARY

- Achilles (AH-kill-ees): King of Phthia, son of Peleus and Thetis, supposedly invulnerable except for his heel
- Aeneas (Ah-knee-ass): Son of Anchises and the goddess Aphrodite, warrior of Troy
- Aeolia (Ay-oh-lee-ah): Island of Aeolus
- Aeolus (Ay-oh-luss): God of the winds
- Aesimus (Ay-see-muss): Father of Sinon
- Agamemnon (Ag-ah-mem-non): King of Mycenae, brother of Menelaus, post-powerful ruler in Greece
- Agelaus (Ag-ee-l-ow-uss): Servant of King Priam
- Ajax (Ay-jacks): The largest, strongest hero on the Greek side, second only to Achilles
- Alkimos (Al-kee-moos): Crewman of Odysseus
- Amazons (Am-MAH-zons): Race of warrior women
- Amphialos (Am-fee-ah-loss): Crewman of Odysseus
- Amphidamas (Am-fee-dah-mass): Crewman of Odysseus
- Amphinomus (Am-fee-no-muss): One of the Suitors
- Anchises (An-k-eye-sees): Father of Aeneas
- Antinous (An-tee-noos): One of the Suitors

Glossary

- Aphrodite (AFF-row-die-tee): Goddess of love, mother of Aeneas
- Apollo (APP-oll-oh): God of music, archery, and healing
- Ares (AIR-rees): God of war
- Artemis (Arr-tem-iss): Goddess of the moon and hunting
- Ascanius (Ass-cah-knee-uss): Son of Aeneas and Creusa
- Athene (Ath-EE-knee): Goddess of war, wisdom, and craft
- Aulis (Ow-liss): Port-town near Mycenae, on the eastern coast of the Greek mainland.
- Bryseis (Bre-say-iss): A Trojan girl enslaved by Achilles.
- Calchas (Cal-cass): Prophet on the Greek side
- Calypso (Cal-ip-so): A nymph; daughter of the Titan Atlas; lives on Ogygia
- Cassandra (Cass-AN-dr-ahh): Princess of Troy, sister of Hector, Paris, and Deiphobus
- Charybdis (Car-rib-diss): A monstrous whirlpool in the Straits of Darkness
- Chryseis (Cre-say-iss): Daughter of Chryses, enslaved by Agamemnon.
- Chryses (Cry-sees): Priest of Apollo, father of Chryseis
- Circe (Sir-see): A witch
- Clytemnestra (Cl-eye-tem-ness-trah): Wife of Agamemnon, queen of Mycenae

- Creusa (Cr-ay-oo-sah): Wife of Aeneas
- Cyprus (SIGH-pruss): Island in the south of Greece, home of Aphrodite
- Deiphobus (Day-iff-oh-buss): Brother of Hector and Paris, son of Priam and Hecuba
- Diomedes (Die-oh-mee-dees): Greek warrior, third strongest on the Greek side
- Eris (Air-riss): Goddess of discord and strife
- Erymanthian (air-REE-man-thee-an): Area of Greece
- Eumaeus (You-may-uss): Swineherd of Ithaca
- Eurycleia (Yur-ree-clay-ah): Old nurse of Telemachus
- Eurylochus (Yur-ree-lock-uss): Brother-in-law and second in command to Odysseus
- Eurymachus (Yur-ree-mach-uss): One of the Suitors
- Hector (Heck-torr): Eldest son of Priam and Hecuba, prince of Troy, the greatest Trojan warrior
- Hecuba (Heck-you-baa): Queen of Troy, wife of Priam, mother of Hector, Paris, Cassandra, and Deiphobus
- Helen (Hell-en): Daughter of Tyndareus and Leda of Sparta, wife of Menelaus
- Helios (Hell-ee-oss): The titan who pulled the sun across the sky with his chariot
- Hellespont (Hell-ess-pont): Strait of water near Troy, joining the Black Sea and the Mediterranean
- Hera (HERE-rah): Queen of the gods
- Herakles (HAIR-rah-kl-ees): Son of Zeus and a mortal woman, had superhuman strength.

Glossary

- Hesione (Hess-EE-oh-knee): Sister of Priam
- Hydra (Hi-draa): A monster with several heads
- Ida (EYE-da): Mountain near Troy
- Ilium (Ill-EE-um): Land around Troy
- Iphigenia (Ih-fidge-en-eye-ah): Daughter of Agamemnon and Clytemnestra
- Ithaca (Ih-THA-cah): Island in the west of Greece, home of Odysseus
- Laertes (Lay-err-tees): Father of Odysseus
- Laocoon (L-ow-oc-oo-on): Priest of Apollo
- Laomedon (Lay-OH-me-don): King of Troy, father of Priam
- Leda (Lay-dah): Wife of Tyndareus, mother of Helen
- Lernea (Lerr-nay-ah): Area of Greece
- Lycaon (Lie-cah-on): Crewman of Odysseus
- Melantho (Mel-an-tho): Maid of Penelope
- Menelaus (Men-uh-LAY-us): king of Sparta and younger son of Atreus, king of Mycenae; the abduction of his wife, Helen, led to the Trojan War.
- Moly (Moh-lee): A poisonous plant
- Mycenae (My-see-knee): City in Greece
- Myrmidons (Murr-mid-on-ss): Warriors of Phthia, supposedly transformed from ants into men.
- Nemean (Knee-me-an): Area of Greece
- Nestor (Ness-torr): The oldest of the Greek kings, king of Pylos, advisor to Agamemnon
- Odysseus (Oh-DISS-ee-uhs): King of Ithaca, husband of Penelope, father of Telemachus

- Ogygia (Og-gi-gee-ah): Island home of Calypso
- Olympus (OH-limm-puss): Mountain home of the gods
- Palamedes (Pal-ah-mee-dees): Messenger of Agamemnon
- Palastor (Pall-ass-torr): Advisor to Menelaus and Helen
- Paris (PAH-riss): Son of King Priam of Troy
- Patroclus (Puh-TROH-cluss): Friend of Achilles
- Peleus (Pell-ay-uss): Mortal grandson of Zeus, husband of Thetis, father of Achilles
- Penelope (Pen-ell-oh-pee): Wife of Odysseus, mother of Telemachus
- Phaeacians (Fee-ay-sions): City of sailors
- Philoctetes (Fill-oc-tee-tees): Greek archer, former companion of Herakles
- Philoetius (Fill-oi-tee-uss): Cowherd of Ithaca
- Phthia (PUH-thee-ah): City in Greece, home of Achilles
- Polites (Po-lie-tees): Crewman of Odysseus
- Polyphemus (Poll-ee-fee-muss): Cyclops, a one-eyed giant, son of Poseidon
- Poseidon (Poss-EYE-don): God of the sea, father of Polyphemus
- Priam (Pry-am): King of Troy, son of Laomedon, father of Hector, Paris, Cassandra, and Deiphobus
- Protesilaus (Pro-tess-ih-lay-uss): Young Greek warrior from Ithaca
- Sarpedon (Sarr-pee-don): Trojan warrior

Glossary

- Scaean (Sky-an): A set of gates at Troy.
- Scylla (SILL-uh): A long-necked monster living across from Charybdis
- Sinon (Sigh-non): The Greek warrior left behind to tell the Trojans about the Wooden Horse
- Sirens (Sigh-rens): Winged women whose singing lures men to their island
- Skyros (Sky-ross): City in Greece near Phthia
- Sparta (SPAR-tuh): City in the Peloponnese, southern area of Greece
- Styx (Sticks): The river which flows around the Underworld
- Telamon (Tell-a-mon): Friend and helper of Herakles
- Telemachus (Tell-eh-ma-cuss): Son of Odysseus and Penelope
- Teucer (Tyoo-sir): Brother of Ajax
- Thetis (THEE-tiss): sea nymph, wife of Peleus, mother of Achilles
- Tiresias (Tie-ree-see-ass): A blind prophet from Thebes
- Troy (Tr-oi): City in Asia
- Tyndareus (Tin-DAH-ree-uss): King of Sparta, father of Helen
- Zeus (Zoos): King of the Gods

Milton Keynes UK
Ingram Content Group UK Ltd.
UKHW020636110124
435856UK00016B/434